NOTES FROM THE COACH

The Power of the Pro-Vision™ Life

Ed Cerny, Ph.D
with Margaret Locklair

Steve, 7/12/10

Thanks for being real &.

Coach

Pro 3:5-6

Coach's Corner Press
148 Citadel Dr.
Conway, SC 29526

Dedication

To Ernie, who has allowed me the freedom to write.
Margaret

To Bill Solomon, my mentor & friend.
Ed

For more information, please contact.
The Coach's Corner Press
148 Citadel Dr.
Conway, SC 29526
or phone 1-800-681-4231

Cover Photo by Bob Dalto, Photographics
Cover & Content Design by W. Bryan Mroz, Print Master

Bible Quotes from New International Version

ISBN 0-9661020-0-2

Printing provided by
Publishers Express Press
P.O. Box 123
Ladysmith, WI 54848
1-800-255-9929

TABLE OF CONTENTS

Chapter

Chapter 1
Player Comes Before Coach

At eight years old I was already well aware that, to the average Little League coach, I looked like a poor candidate for an athlete.

My glasses were half an inch thick — compliments of a case of the mumps when I was two. My right leg was shorter, smaller and weaker than my left — the result of surviving polio when I was four. But with three younger brothers to contend with, I was tougher than I looked, and I loved any game played with a ball. The trick was finding a coach long-suffering enough to show me how.

There were coaches who never gave me a chance. There were some who tried to teach me and quit. In the middle of a hotly contested high school varsity game, there was the football coach who called for a player and who, when I jumped off the bench, knocked me backwards with a strong forearm, shouting, "Not you. I mean a *real* player!"

Something kept me coming back, even as a solid resolve was taking shape in my mind. If I ever — ever! — had the chance to coach a team, I would approach it differently. I would search for the smallest thing that even my poorest player did right. I would seize on it, build on it. I would make absolutely certain that player had the encouragement to keep on

Player's Box

trying. I would make these games what they were supposed to be: a way of growing up healthy in body, mind, and spirit.

In the meantime, I still wanted to play. After being cut from my high school football team as a junior, I spent the off-season building myself up, and by the second game of my senior year, I had become a starter. In the mid-60's, I achieved my goal of making the football team at the University of Kentucky. Later, I'll tell the story of why I never played.

Today, though, I look back on having earned the rank of Eagle Scout, a Ph.D., and a wealth of experiences in a wide-ranging career, and realize I've approached most of these challenges as a coach. That includes five years working in fitness centers, 12 years as a college faculty member, and the founding in 1995 of The Coach's Corner, a motivational consulting firm to businesses, corporations and governmental agencies. I've spent my happiest hours, however, in actual coaching time — some of it paid and some volunteer, working with guys and girls of a wide range of ages, from youth league to high school to college level.

My coaching methods work, though they didn't hatch full-grown. They've developed over time. When I first started coaching, I was focused only on winning. I understood the fundamentals of mechanics, but I had a lot to learn about people and motivation.

Over the years, however, I've developed a philosophy that

Player's Box

reaches much farther into the lives of my "players" — whether athletic, academic or corporate — than do the temporary gains won by properly executing a play, or posting a win on the scoreboard or in the boardroom.

I know this because so many of my former players and students and seminar attendees keep in touch. I get letters and phone calls and e-mail from people I haven't seen in years. When something goes right in their lives, they want me to know. When something goes wrong, they want me to help put things into perspective. By the grace of God, I have been given a gift of encouragement, and there is no greater pleasure for me than to use it.

Encouragement, I've learned, doesn't mean looking only at the positive. The negative has to be identified and called by name. But dwelling on the negative is pointless. It is the pro-active lifestyle that develops a pro. Becoming a pro, becoming excellent, is my desire for everyone I work with. Why are we so content to be something less? In a world full of options, it's the ability to focus your life that enables you to squeeze the most from it. Ultimately, it all comes down to the ability to press toward a goal, an excellent goal, refusing to stop until you get there.

That's what these notes from the coach are intended to help you to do: live like a pro. Though you and I may never work together on an athletic field, I can teach you how to focus your

Player's Box

3

life to get the most out of it — to maximize the talents you were born with. I can coach you through a set of broad-based principles that will help you produce excellence.

Most of the chapters in this book are divided into segments analogous to those a coach uses to teach his players. These segments correspond to an old maxim that guides much of my own coaching and teaching. It goes:

> I hear, I forget.
> I see, I remember.
> I do, I understand.

Each chapter is introduced by a **"CHALK TALK"** — my explanation of a particular principle. Next, the chapter looks at how real people live out the principle in the section entitled **"STUDYING THE CLIPS."** You execute the principle yourself in the section entitled "Stretching Exercise." The book has been designed to include group study, too. After you have completed your individual **"STRETCHING EXERCISES,"** you can go on to **"TEAM EXERCISES."** Putting these plays into practice is essential to your success, and as the proverb explains so succinctly, you will not understand until you put feet on the principle and actually apply it. We've also added the "Player's Box" at the bottom of each page. This allows the reader to add points of his own based on what he has read. We

Player's Box

4

encourage you to use this box as a way of capturing creative thoughts. Finally, we close each chapter with a "FOCAL POINT."

FOCAL POINT:
"May the favor of the Lord our God rest upon us: establish the work of our hands for us — yes, establish the work of our hands." Psalm 90:17

Player's Box

Chapter 2
The Pro-Vision™

THE CHALK TALK:

Tucked in my wallet, there's a $100 bill that I've tried dozens of times to give away. So far, not a single person has met my one prerequisite for claiming it. As I meet with the CEO of a company, the preliminaries usually go like this:

"Do you have a mission statement?" I ask.

"Yes."

"Who wrote it?"

"I did."

"Do your employees know what it says?"

"Oh, yes. We make sure every one of them reads it. They have to initial it once they've finished."

"Good." I pull out my wallet, extract Ben Franklin, unfold him and stretch the bill full width. "I'll give you this $100 bill," I offer, "if you can tell me exactly what your mission statement and core values say, verbatim."

There hasn't been a single winner yet. Nor do I expect one, as long as CEOs and other executives consider the mission statement the end-all of corporate identity and direction.

What's the problem with a mission statement? Nothing whatsoever, as long as the employees (1) know what it says,

Player's Box

6

(2) believe in it, and (3) live it. But how many employees can recite the contents of a single-spaced document that typically ranges a full page or more in length?

"Well," the execs frequently counter, "they understand the meat of it. That's what counts." But do they really understand it? So far, not a single employee has won my hundred dollars, either, and I've offered it to hundreds of them. In fact, only the choicest handful could recite even a single point in the company's mission statement.

To be a pro at anything, you have to know where you're going. You focus. You establish the direction in which you're heading, and you move deliberately in that precise direction.

Just because you're busy does not mean that you know where you're going. A busy life is not necessarily a focused life. You can be wildly busy, wheels spinning all the time, and be getting nowhere. If you leave Atlanta planning to arrive in Miami, and drive 65 miles an hour heading northeast, you're making great time, but you're still going in the wrong direction. Your intent was to go to Miami, not New York.

No, a pro has a clear vision of where he's going and how to get there. Every one of us needs such a Pro-Vision™, both for our companies and for ourselves as individuals.

A Pro-Vision™ is a summary statement of identity and purpose that has heart and passion — two characteristics usually absent from the mission statement. A Pro-Vision™

Player's Box

sums up the very guts of what you're about. It's succinct — 10 words or less — the shorter the better, for ease in remembering it. And you have to be able to remember it — all day long. You have to keep that Pro-Vision™ constantly in front of you to keep from being sidetracked.

STUDYING THE CLIPS:

I first encountered a Pro-Vision™ when I joined the Scouts, though we called it a motto. "Be Prepared" — it doesn't get much more succinct than that. But what a phenomenal amount of meat that included! Soon I learned that unless I wanted to subsist on raw potatoes again, I had to pack my own wax-coated matches for a camp-out. Be prepared! I learned — again the hard way — to take my own groundcloth to put under my tent, rather than relying on the other fellows to bring one. Being prepared sure beat sleeping in a wet sleeping bag.

Those two words don't begin to sum up everything I learned during my years of Scouting. But those two words do sum up the reason I was acquiring those qualities and skills. I was being prepared to think ahead — not to ramble aimlessly through life, but to succeed in this tough world. Being prepared helped me stay focused on achieving my goal of becoming an Eagle Scout. I still think about that Pro-Vision™ statement almost every day, and act on it.

Companies that take the time to distill their goals into a

Player's Box

8

Pro-Vision™ statement and then diligently teach it to their employees, day in and day out, find themselves moving toward something others will recognize as distinctive.

What do you think of, for example, when you hear the words "Federal Express"? The word "overnight" pops into mind for me. FedEx has built a corporate image. Give them a properly addressed package by a certain time, and they'll deliver it by a designated time — often the next day. Though they may not call it that, FedEx has a terrific Pro-Vision™ statement: "The World On Time."

Imagine the effect on FedEx's employees to hear that slogan every day. It means that every single letter or packet they handle has to get to its destination on time, no matter where in the world it is going.

"The World On Time." It's punchy. It's tough. It's passionate. It's easy to remember. Properly taught and reinforced, that Pro-Vision™ statement should be the driving force behind every single action a FedEx employee takes. Theirs is a company of people who know where they're going.

Corporate America gives us a number of other excellent examples of successful Pro-Vision™ statements. If you've ever stayed at a Ritz-Carlton Hotel and experienced that company's dignified style of guest relations, you'll recognize what I would describe as the Ritz' Pro-Vision™: "We are ladies and gentlemen serving ladies and gentlemen." That says

Player's Box

it all.

Walt Disney was a family man, a dad who took his little girls to an amusement park on weekends and was bothered by the park's peeling exterior and the broken horses on the merry-go-round. What I would call his initial Pro-Vision™ for Disneyland was: "A place where all the horses jump and there's no chipped paint." Over the years, as the Disney empire expanded, the Pro-Vision™ became more focused, yet more inclusive. Today, they sum it up in three words: "We Create Happiness." We won't debate the illusory qualities of happiness, or whether such a state can actually be achieved by a visit to Disney. The point is that, behind the actions of every employee, from the CEO to the sweeper, there's a motivating force: make the guest happy.

The Hallmark Company's Pro-Vision™ could be found inside its extremely effective marketing slogan: "When you care enough to send the very best." If I were the human resource director at Hallmark, I would make sure those last three words were reinforced in the mind of each employee in every way possible. "We hire the very best," I would tell them. "That means you are the very best. And you produce the very best."

Nike has a ready-made Pro-Vision™ statement in its advertising slogan "Just Do It." It can motivate employees as well as buyers as well as wearers, and it drives the competition crazy!

Jesus had a precisely defined Pro-Vision™. We could

Player's Box

condense it as "Doing The Father's Will." No matter which New Testament gospel you read, you never see Jesus veering from the purpose summed up in John 4:38: His Father had sent Him, and He was here to do the will of His Father. He never once stepped outside of His Pro-Vision™ — from the early days of His ministry, when He taught His disciples to pray, "Our Father ... Thy will be done...," to His final hours, when He prayed, "Not my will but thine be done."

I repeat: to be a pro at anything, you have to know where you're going. You have to establish the direction you're heading, clear out the obstacles, and move forward with single-minded purpose. This book is written for the person who wants to become a pro, not the one satisfied with simply letting life happen to him.

Player's Box

STRETCHING EXERCISE ONE:

Ask yourself, "What is my Pro-Vision™ for my personal life?"
Who am I working to be every day? Am I aiming for something specific or am I wandering?" This may take several
hours or several days to distill. Write down your thoughts as
they come. When you see a direction, summarize it in 10
words or less. You'll be introduced to my own Pro-Vision™ in
Chapter 4.

STRETCHING EXERCISE TWO:

If you own a business, or plan to start one, ask yourself,
"What is the Pro-Vision™ of my business? What do I want
every employee of my business to work toward?" Remember
how Scouting, FedEx, Disney, Hallmark and Nike have all
succeeded by combining a high quality product with a pithy
Pro-Vision™ statement that every employee can keep upper-
most in mind. Keep your Pro-Vision™ to 10 words or less.
Write it down.

Before sharing it with your company teammates, have them
go through the same exercise and see what they come up with.
Then compare and compromise for a Team Pro-Vision™.

TEAM STRETCHING EXERCISE ONE:

In your group meeting, share the Pro-Vision™ each of you
has created for your own personal life. Also, share how this is
making a difference in your life. Or is it?

Player's Box

TEAM STRETCHING EXERCISE TWO:

Share the Pro-Vision™ your company has developed. What will have to take place for it to work? Use examples.

FOCAL POINT:

"'For I know the plans I have for you,' declares the Lord, 'plans to prosper you and not to harm you, plans to give you a hope and a future.'" Jeremiah 29:11

Player's Box

Chapter 3
The Pro-Values™

THE CHALK TALK:

Anyone who establishes a Pro-Vision™ has a second challenge to tackle immediately. He has to decide how to achieve it, specifically deciding which values will shape his pursuit of the Pro-Vision™. To ignore this can actually be dangerous, especially if you're in business and employ people who haven't learned to read your mind.

Consider a hypothetical overnight delivery firm we'll name "Nightwing." Suppose Nightwing held a company-wide meeting to announce its Pro-Vision™ of "Committed to Delivery on Schedule." Imagine that corporate leadership failed to teach the company's drivers that they must be courteous at the same time that they are being firm in adhering to their pick-up schedule.

Here's the scenario: a customer rushes to a drop box waving a sheaf of papers just as a driver prepares to pull off. The customer has no label prepared for his package. Conscious of the Pro-Vision™, the driver bellows, "I can't wait," and leaves the outraged customer in the exhaust, making a solemn vow to do business with a competitor forever after.

Fortunately for Nightwing, its values were thought out ahead of time. Drivers were trained to be as courteous and helpful as possible: to give the customer an envelope, a ship-

Player's Box

14

ping label, and the location of the next pickup box or Nightwing office so he can go there directly. But the driver must also be firm. "No," he must be able to say, "I cannot wait for you to fill out the label. It will put me behind schedule, and at Nightwing, we're committed to delivery on schedule."

Courtesy, helpfulness, and uncompromising commitment to a deadline are three Pro-Values™ a company like Nightwing would demand of its employees if they're serious about achieving the Pro-Vision™.

As a boy, because my ability to play sports was hampered, I threw myself into Scouting, adopting the organization's Pro-Vision™ as my own. But how was I to conduct myself as I learned to Be Prepared?

The founders of Scouting had already thought through the question. No, they did not want me to Be Prepared by stealing someone else's pocket knife when I lost my own. A Scout should be trustworthy. They did not want me to Be Prepared to run away from danger when it was within my power to help someone. A Scout should be brave.

And so the Scouting Fathers settled on 12 attributes a model Scout should incorporate into his personality. These 12 attributes were drilled into us; we memorized and recited them. "A Scout is trustworthy. A Scout is loyal. A Scout is helpful ... friendly ... courteous ... kind ...obedient ... cheerful ... thrifty ... brave ... clean ... reverent."

Player's Box

Those are Pro-Values™. Learning them taught me how to keep the Scout oath, which serves as the equivalent of a good mission statement: "On my honor I will do my best to do my duty to God and my country, and to obey the Scout law, to help other people at all times, to keep myself physically strong, mentally awake and morally straight." As long as I exemplified the 12 values, I was doing my best. And all of it was teaching me to Be Prepared.

Within these elements, then, lies the formula for personal and corporate identity: (1) A terse, pithy, passionate Pro-Vision™ that you can immediately bring to mind a hundred times a day, if necessary, to keep you focused. (2) A precisely thought-out list of Pro-Values™ that says what you stand for.

STUDYING THE CLIPS:

Back when John R. Wooden, the legendary winner of 10 NCAA championships, was head basketball coach at UCLA, he drew up a diagram for his players called "The Pyramid of Success." It is made up of tiers of blocks, 35 in all. Each block contains what I call a Pro-Value™, those attributes that contribute to success.

"Industriousness," for example, is one of the pyramid's cornerstones. Beneath that word is Wooden's explanation:

Player's Box

"There is no substitute for work. Worthwhile things come from hard work and careful planning."

Someone climbing John Wooden's pyramid would come to such values as self-control, skill, intentness, honesty, initiative and faith on his way to the vertex, which is labeled "competitive greatness." The word "SUCCESS" — which I would call the Pro-Vision™ — rests like a crown on top. John Wooden is a man who knows precisely how to attain the success that crowns the pyramid of values he taught his players. Today at 87 he is a living example of his Pro-Vision™.

In the mid-1990's, the Disney Corporation adopted controversial changes in corporate policy that focused public attention on its values. Decades before, however, Disney set out a clearly defined set of Pro-Values™ (though they don't call them by that name) which taught employees how to treat patrons.

Safety is Disney's number one value — not only for guests but also for employees, otherwise known as "cast members." A second key Disney value is courtesy. If, for example, someone asks a cast member a question he cannot answer, he is trained not to respond, "I don't know," but instead to say, "That's a very good question, sir or ma'am. Let's go find out the answer together," or "Wait right here and I'll find out for you."

A third value is professionalism. (Disney refers to this as "The Show.") Cast members are trained to think of themselves

Player's Box

as being either "on stage" — where their every move is intended to enhance the visit of their guests — or "off stage," meaning they're on break, out of sight of the guests. Should a guest experience a "tragic moment" as opposed to a "magic moment," cast members are taught that they have a small window of opportunity in which to turn the moment around. They are diligently taught to seize that moment.

The last key Disney value is efficiency, stressing the necessity of being efficient in everything they do.

I've found that people have an easier time remembering their Pro-Values™ if they tie them to an acronym related to their Pro-Vision™. I often conduct seminars for the fast growing resort city of Myrtle Beach, SC. City leaders decided their goal was to provide outstanding service. They chose the statement "First in Service" as their Pro-Vision™.

With the employees, we talked about the values they should possess to achieve that Pro-Vision™ of being first in service. The employees themselves were easily able to identify those values and tie them into the word "service." The finished list reads like this:

<table>
<tr><td>Player's Box</td></tr>
</table>

18

S - safety, both for yourself and those you serve.
E - excellence in everything. Aim to constantly improve.
R - respect yourself and others.
V - value the individual and the organization.
I - integrity. Practice fairness and honesty.
C - courtesy and communication, to all and with all.
E - education. Have the knowledge you need to help.

The City printed an ID card the size of an average business card. On the front is the Pro-Vision™ "First in Service" and on the back is the acronym spelling out the Pro-Values™. Every single city employee, from the person who cleans the recycling center to the policeman on the beat, from the clerk of court to the city manager, should be carrying that card, reminding them that they're working toward the same goal — and using the same set of values to get there.

By looking at what Jesus identified as the greatest commandments, we can easily see a Pro-Vision™, backed up perfectly by a set of supporting Pro-Values™ that tell us how to achieve it. God gave us the Pro-Vision™ as a two-parter:
> (1) to love God with all of our heart, soul, mind and strength (Deut. 6:5 and Matt. 22:37)
> (2) to love our neighbors as we love ourselves. (Lev. 19:18 and Matt. 22:39)

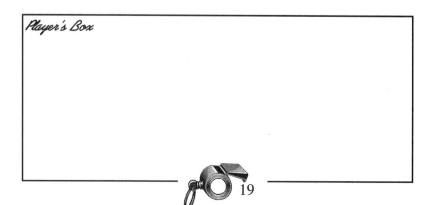

Player's Box

Immediately, the question arises: exactly how do we practice this love of God and neighbor? Can we do it, as have many cultures throughout history, by "loving" a temple prostitute as we offer sacrifices on an altar made in the image of a mighty animal? Today, that may seem an extreme or ridiculous example, but the point is that men and women, left to our own imagination, will always devise our own means of achieving a Pro-Vision™.

Instead, God gave us a set of Pro-Values™ to accomplish the Pro-Vision™. We know them as the Ten Commandments. For the record, God commands us:

(1) to give no person and no thing a higher place in our hearts than He holds. (You shall have no other gods before me.)

(2) to make no physical representation of Him, since nothing on earth can adequately portray His glory. (You shall not make any graven image ... you shall not bow down to it, or worship it.)

(3) to speak of Him only in reverence and truth. (You shall not take the name of the Lord your God in vain.)

(4) to use His Sabbath Day as the gift He intends it to be, by spending time with Him and resting. (Remember the Sabbath Day and keep it holy. Six days shall you labor and do all your work ...)

Note that these first four commandments tell us how to love

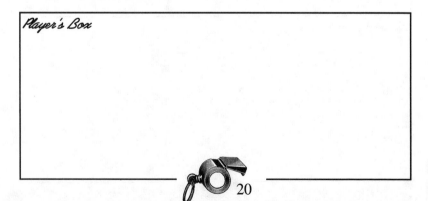

Player's Box

God; the next six tell us how to love our neighbor.

(5) to honor your father and mother.

(6) to refuse to murder.

(7) to refuse to commit sexual sins.

(8) to refuse to steal.

(9) to refuse to lie against someone else.

(10) to refuse to covet those things that belong to someone else.

In John 14:15, Jesus says, "If you love me (that's part one of His Pro-Vision) keep my commandments" (those are the Pro-Values.)

Player's Box

STRETCHING EXERCISE:

With your Pro-Vision™ constantly before you, develop your own set of Pro-Values™, either for your personal life, your business, or both. If at all possible, create an acronym that will help you remember your Pro-Values™.

TEAM STRETCHING EXERCISE:

Discuss in your group how establishing Pro-Values™ has made a difference in your life - personally and/or professionally. Is there power in Pro-Values™? Why or why not?

FOCAL POINT:

"As iron sharpens iron, so one man sharpens another."
Proverbs 27:17

Player's Box

Chapter 4
The Coach's Corner

THE CHALK-TALK:

Few things bother me as much as a coach who fails to follow his own training guidelines. You've seen him — the guy who makes his team run wind-sprints for conditioning while he crosses his arms over his bulging stomach. Or the coach who preaches fitness from inside a cloud of smoke. I knew a college coach who was careful to remind his players that they served as role models for their fans. The coach himself, however, was twice arrested for drunk driving.

A good coach — whether on the playing field, the factory floor, in the corporate boardroom or the family den — must believe in the Pro-Vision™ he lays out for his team. He must establish and teach the rules by which his players will operate. Ultimately, his actions must prove that he, himself, lives by those same beliefs and rules.

STUDYING THE CLIPS:

Yes, I practice what I preach. I operate by two Pro-Visions™: one for my personal life and one for my company, The Coach's Corner. I list them in that order for a reason. Life is far, far more than a career, and I am far, far

Player's Box

more than my business. The personal Pro-Vision™ must outrank, shape and, in some cases, dictate the professional one — never the other way around. My career is important to me, but in order for it to be an integrated part of my life, my professional Pro-Vision™ must fit seamlessly into my personal Pro-Vision™ which is: "Do all to the glory of God." It comes from a passage in the Bible, specifically I Corinthians 10:31. To learn why I chose that, please see my personal testimony in the final chapter.

I tie my Pro-Values™ to the acronym C.O.A.C.H., since that word sums up my approach to both my personal and my professional life.

C = Christ-Centered
O = Opportunity to Witness
A = All-Star
C = Congratulate
H = Healthy

Let's look at why I chose each of those five values.

<u>Christ-Centered</u> - Although I am the head coach of The Coach's Corner, Jesus Christ is the owner of the business. Just as the coach of a professional sports team must follow the priorities set by the owner, I must follow the priorities of my owner, who is Christ. In my life, the Lord comes first, my family second, and my work third. Knowing this makes it

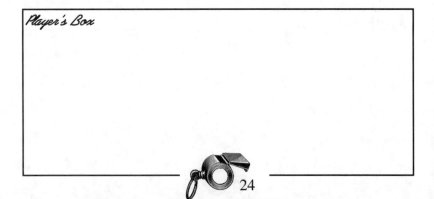

Player's Box

easier to make decisions.

Opportunity to Witness - Each day the Lord gives me opportunities to witness about what He has done in my life. I have a choice of deciding whether to speak up or be silent. As a coach, I must speak out because I might be the only "Bible" a particular person ever sees.

All-Star - is an abbreviated way for me to remember that I am to do my best at all times. I want to be one of God's All-Stars, keeping in mind the admonition in Colossians 3:23: "And whatsoever you do, do it heartily, as to the Lord, and not unto men."

Congratulate - The Bible helped me identify encouragement as my primary spiritual gift, and I use the word "congratulate" to remind me to exercise this gift whenever possible. Sometimes, I encourage people by "catching" them doing things well, allowing me to congratulate them. Just as often, though, encouragement involves drawing alongside someone who is discouraged and giving him a jumpstart.

Healthy - To accomplish the other values in my life, I must recognize that the Holy Spirit lives within my body, and therefore I must take care of my body by controlling what I eat and

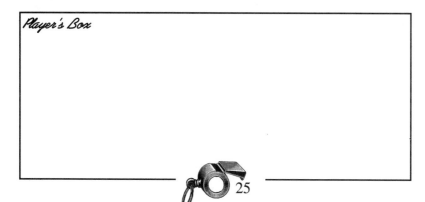

Player's Box

drink, the distress I put myself under, and the amount of rest and exercise I get. Basically, how I choose to take care of myself will have a marked effect on my performance as a player/coach on the Lord's team.

Those, then, are the five Pro-Values™ that govern how I will work to accomplish my personal Pro-Vision™: "Do All to the Glory of God."

Next, let's consider the focus for my business. Here, my Pro-Vision™ is "Building Leaders, Achieving Goals." I believe that while some leaders are born, leadership skills can be cultivated in everyone, and most of us can and do lead in one or more spheres of life. Leaders are goal-oriented people, who not only set goals but achieve them. As I consult with clients, I stress the importance of actually achieving those goals we spend such a long time identifying. Again, I tie my Pro-Values™ to the word C.O.A.C.H.

C = Corporate Cultural Cheerleader
O = Opportunity to Grow
A = All-Star
C = Congratulate
H = Healthy

Corporate Cultural Cheerleader - Every business has its own corporate culture, and within that culture, people tend to

Player's Box

factionalize. In industries, for example, the manufacturing employees and the marketing employees often tend to look at one another with suspicion. My goal is to bring all factions together. Mutual understanding and mutual goal-setting can produce a team, not a band of warring factions.

<u>Opportunity to Grow</u> - Originally, I called this the opportunity to fail, but later felt that was too negative. We all know we haven't grown without making mistakes, and without taking calculated risks. This Pro-Value™ reminds me to ask myself what kinds of things I should do each day to become a better business person.

<u>All-Star</u> - My goal is to help my clients and their employees learn what it takes to be an all-star employee on the corporate team, rather than simply meeting the minimum requirements. Too often, people come to work just to get a paycheck rather than to use their talents and really enjoy working. It doesn't have to be that way.

<u>Congratulate</u> - Too many managers refuse to acknowledge their employees' good work. Let's say a receptionist does an exceptional job of answering the phone, but no one in the office thanks her for it. They say, "Well, that's what she gets paid to do." That's wrong. We need to congratulate people on doing

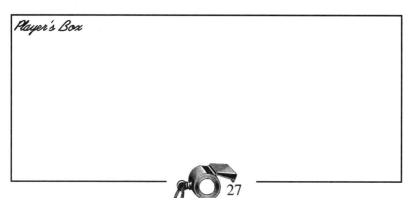

Player's Box

the little things well. They will take pride in what they do and begin taking on bigger projects with confidence. I work to set the example.

<u>Healthy</u> - Both at work and at home, a productive, satisfied employee is going to have a healthy approach to six critical areas of life. I discuss each of the six in subsequent chapters of this book.

These two sets of Pro-Visions™ not only show you who I am — through my personal and professional values — but also keep me focused.

Player's Box

STRETCHING EXERCISE:

Now that you have seen my personal and professional visions and values, review those you formulated after reading chapters two and three. Answer this: if someone asked me what my values are, could I answer him without pulling out a sheet of paper? Could I answer from my heart? Are my values a living, breathing part of me? If not, do these exercises again.

TEAM STRETCHING EXERCISE:

In discussing this Pro-Vision™, Pro-Value™ system, ask: "Why is it so hard for people to make a change?"

FOCAL POINT:

"Whether you turn to the right or to the left, your ears will hear a voice behind you, saying, 'This is the way; walk in it.'" Isaiah 30:21

Player's Box

Chapter 5
Identifying the Obstacles

THE CHALK TALK:

Cross your arms and notice which arm you automatically placed on top. Now cross them the other way. Uncomfortable, isn't it? Fairly early in life, you established a habit of crossing your arms in a particular way, and now it's automatic.

That's not the only habit you established. We each have dozens of them, some strengths and some weaknesses, depending on what they contribute to the pursuit of our Pro-Vision™. Habits can either be your greatest ally or your most relentless enemy.

Do you routinely get to work on time? If so, that's probably the result of dozens of tiny habits you've established that range from faithfully setting the alarm clock each night to denying yourself the pleasure of reading the entire newspaper during breakfast. You routinely say "yes" to taking a shower and "no" to playing a round of golf before work — and you practice these habits habitually because you truly believe it's important to get to work on time.

The key word here is "believe." Millions of people give lip-service to being on time. They acknowledge its importance, but they're late anyway. Actions, then, really do speak louder than words. If you're consistently late, you don't really believe

Player's Box

it's important to be on time; otherwise, you would be. If people truly, genuinely, believe something is important, they will do it. To do it, they establish rules or guidelines for themselves, say "no" to distractions, and work to establish habits that are distinctively Pro-Vision™.

Habits are essential to life. They free us from having to make incessant mundane decisions. They free our minds to think about more challenging and interesting things than — for example — how to accurately place your tennis serve. You don't want to have to think through every step of a serve every time you play tennis. Instead, you want serving to become a useful habit, so your focus can be on scoring points.

Sociologists tell us that it takes an average of 21 repetitions, at a minimum, to establish a new habit. So, if you're learning a new tennis serve, for example, you have to practice it at least 21 times — and possibly many more than that — to be able to count on it during a game. These same sociologists have found that roughly 100 repetitions are necessary for a habit to become automatic.

After one of my seminars on this subject, given to a number of golf instructors, several approached me looking as if a light bulb just come on. They told me that the 21 Rule also applies in teaching people how to play golf — that when they instruct someone in how to grip the club differently, for example, it takes at least 21 times to become comfortable with the new

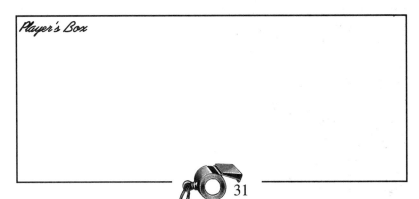

Player's Box

grip. The pros said they had never thought about it before, but it would now be easier for them to make habit changes in their own lives, as well.

Virtually no obstacle is harder to eliminate than a bad habit — I admit that up front. But a pro prays about it, bites the bullet, and works on changing the habit. He denies himself the soft choices. He keeps his Pro-Vision™ in front of him all the time, reminding himself of his focus day after day, hour after hour. That's how lives are changed.

If you are truly committed to your Pro-Vision™, you need to examine yourself for any habits that keep you from living it. Be brutally honest. Are you simply trying to change your actions long enough to achieve a short-term goal, and then slip back into your comfortable old habits? Or are you changing your underlying beliefs — a much more ambitious but highly profitable undertaking?

Two examples will illustrate. People forget that loss of health will adversely affect the way we pursue almost any activity in life. For most, staying healthy is a combination of eating properly, exercising, getting enough rest and minimizing distress.

We each have over 600 muscles in our bodies, and they need daily exercise to maintain health. Countless busy executives know that they would feel better if they exercised, but they don't make time. Two questions: Is exercise important? If it is,

Player's Box

do I make time to do it on a regular basis?

I doubt many people would claim that exercise is unimportant. We all know it is, at least hypothetically. The heart of the issue is how important you believe exercise to be to *you*. If you have never exercised, rarely exercised or only poorly exercised, your belief has to be that exercise is not important *to you!*

You absolutely must come to that reality before you can proceed. Unless your belief changes, actions will not change, at least not on a long-term basis.

It is a lie to say that something is important to you, but that you don't have time to do it. People tell me all the time that they don't have time to exercise or eat properly or read the Bible. To be truthful, they should say, "What you're suggesting to me is not important to me at this time," because you will make time for those things that are truly important to you.

Remember, attitude is nothing more than a habit of thought.

STUDYING THE CLIPS:

Years ago, our next-door neighbor called one evening to tell us she and her husband were getting a divorce. What a shock — we had no clue! As a point of conversation, I suggested she consider coming to the fitness center where Zoe Ann and I worked out. It might be a way of relieving some of the tension she was feeling, and it would give us all an ongoing opportunity for helpful discussion.

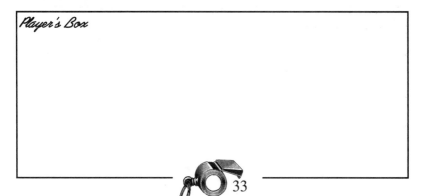

Player's Box

This woman surprised us. She went from no exercise at all to exercising three times a week. At first, I believe, she clung to it like a drowning person clings to a life preserver — it was a way of dealing with incredible distress. But when the distress leveled off, she still stuck to the exercise regimen. Both her actions and her beliefs had changed. She now *believed* that exercise was crucial to her well-being. That was 20 years ago. We still get a Christmas card from her, and she always thanks me for getting her started on the exercise program.

Let me give you a second example of an attempt to change a habit — one that focused on actions but not beliefs. Once I worked for a company that sent its key officers through a motivational/habit-changing program that lasted several weeks.

Among those taking the class was my boss. He was a really nice guy but kept a very messy desk. It was part of his personality; he always knew where to find things on his desktop, but to the untrained eye it was a major disaster. We used to joke about it at the office. He even joked about it, too.

One of the goals he set out to accomplish in the course was to keep a clean desktop. It was a noble goal, involving change of a lifelong habit. Here is how he decided to accomplish it. He moved all of the stuff on his desktop into my office across the hall! He placed it in little piles on the floor along the walls of my office, which had now become his messy desk. Mr. Goal simply wanted to be able to check off at the end of the next

Player's Box

group meeting that he had met his goal. His desktop was clean!

But now, he was forever coming into my office to look for things he needed. From my perspective, the motivational course was a disaster. There was no corporate Pro-Vision™, no personal Pro-Vision™, no thought to changing a belief (he simply switched from "I function best with a messy desk" to "I can still function well with a messy floor.") He changed only an action, not a belief. Without a belief-change, the action will not last. Within a couple of weeks, my boss' desk was as messy as ever.

Positive changes require changing (1) beliefs, (2) rules and (3) actions, in that order. You cannot change an action permanently without changing a belief first. That motivational course was actually into changing actions, not beliefs. My boss needed to reach the point of believing that organization is important to productivity and that it extends further than his desktop. He should have looked at what habits caused him to keep his desk messy. Then he should have established rules to help him keep it neat. (For example: I will divide all of my paperwork into three files marked Today, This Week, and This Month. I will place all magazines and free-time reading material on the bottom shelf of the credenza. I will clean out the desk drawers every Friday afternoon. I will never allow my desk calendar to be covered up by papers.) And then, he should begin to live by his rules.

Player's Box

STRETCHING EXERCISE ONE:

Begin now to list the habits that keep you from unreservedly pursuing or achieving your Pro-Vision™. I suggest you limit your list to five. Identifying them may take you several days of self-observation. But once you've listed five, identify the habit that seems most destructive. Perhaps it's a time-robber. Maybe an energy thief. Maybe it's a question of ethics that weighs on your conscience.Whatever it is, start at the top.

STRETCHING EXERCISE TWO:

Ask yourself the important question: do I truly believe it is important to change this habit? If you conclude that it is, pray about it. If you need to confess something related to this habit, do it now. Ask God for His help in breaking the chains of this habit. Then write down the rules you intend to follow to accomplish this habit-change. Begin immediately to follow your rules. In the days to come, you will need to keep your Pro-Vision™, your Pro-Values™ and your rules constantly in front of you. Remember that it takes at least 21 days or repetitions for a change of action to become a habit. Do not get discouraged if you do not succeed in the first week or even two weeks of attempting to make this habit change. If you blow it, don't beat yourself up about it. Just remind yourself how important this habit change is to you and start again.

Player's Box

TEAM STRETCHING EXERCISE ONE:

Discuss any negative habits common to the group.

TEAM STRETCHING EXERCISE TWO:

Discuss ways you've tried to change a habit. Give examples and encouragement to help each other succeed. Think of ways the group can reinforce the efforts to change both personally and professionally.

FOCAL POINT:

"...they got into the habit of being idle..."   I Timothy 5:13

Player's Box

Chapter 6
Dreams vs. Goals

THE CHALK TALK:

Anybody can set a goal. I am not interested in mere goal-setting. I'm interested in achieving goals — so much so that the Pro-Vision™ for my business is "Building Leaders, Achieving Goals."

What coach or player contents himself with simply *setting a goal* of winning a game? The highest pleasure is in scoring enough points to win! A clean, honest, hard-fought win is one of those thrills you can mentally revisit for the rest of your life. Because the very nature of sports is goal- (post, basket, home plate, finish line, score board) oriented, athletes often have an easier time setting and achieving goals than do non-athletes. Chances are, then, you already have a leg up on grasping the vital nature of goal-setting and goal-achieving.

So many people confuse dreams with goals. You can tell a person is dreaming when he speaks in "Somedays." He may say, "Someday, I'm going to scuba dive," or "Someday, I'll write a book," or "Someday, I'm going to take my family to Europe." Dreaming is essential to goal-setting, but there are specific steps that must be followed if you are actually going to see your dream fulfilled. It always comes back to setting goals.

To live without goals is sometimes compared to Alice's

Player's Box

haphazard journey through Wonderland. Faced with all the rabbit holes, Alice asked the Cheshire Cat, "Would you tell me, please, which way I ought to go from here?" The cat said, "That depends a good deal on where you want to get to." "I don't much care where —," said Alice. "Then it doesn't matter which way you go," said the cat. The title of a book by Dr. David Campbell puts another slant on the same idea: *If You Don't Know Where You're Going, You'll Probably Wind Up Somewhere Else.*

Four steps are necessary to successfully reach a goal. I call them the Four S's. To achieve a goal, you have to:
- See it
- Schedule it
- Start it
- Score it.

Then, if necessary,
- Set it again.

Let's look at these in some detail.

There is nothing mystical about seeing yourself accomplishing a goal. This is not the New-Age technique of visualization, which claims that visualizing an outcome gives you some power to accomplish it. Instead, visualizing prepares you for the hard work to follow. It helps you put the necessary steps in order. And it keeps you going in the face of temptation.

When I taught marketing at Coastal Carolina University, I

Player's Box

always taught my freshmen the importance of picturing them-selves as graduating seniors. They needed to see themselves walking across the stage in their caps and gowns. If, from the first day of class, they could not see themselves graduating, they were far less likely to achieve that goal four years later. Too many lost sight of their goal along the way — drawn away, perhaps, by a job offer or marriage, negative habits or a change in values.

You see, 50 percent of those who enter college never gradu-ate! In fact, less than a quarter of all Americans have a four - year college degree. I contend that if you're smart enough to get into most colleges, you're smart enough to graduate. The reason more students don't is that they fail to set the right goals and follow through.

Scheduling your goals may be one of the most frequently overlooked parts of the goal-setting process. I told my fresh-man marketing students that, not only did they need to be able to see themselves capped and gowned, with diploma in hand, but they also needed to have the month and the year of their graduation firmly planted in their minds.

Scheduling truly separates a dream from a goal. Scheduling is not a "Someday" exercise, but an actual get-out-the-calendar exercise, in which you select and record the date by which you plan to accomplish your goal. It is important to actually write down the goal, along with the completion date, on a 3 x 5 note

Player's Box

card. Next, you need to write down the steps that will be necessary to reach your goal. Then set a completion date for each step, recording all of this on the 3 x 5 card, which you will now carry with you everywhere you go.

Taking this action will help you stay focused. When you're faced with a decision between two attractive alternatives, looking at the card can help you make the choice that will get you closer to your goal.

Starting is easy for some people and difficult for others — particularly people who are afraid of failure. Without risk there is no growth, which is really what life is about. Failure is a vital part of that growing experience, constantly coexisting with success. Failure, in some form, is virtually a daily occurrence for most of us. But some people are simply paralyzed by the fear of it. For the ultimate example of how success coexists with failure, look at the baseball icon Babe Ruth. Few people remember that the Home Run King was also the simultaneous Strike-Out King of his day. Taking a dream out of your head and making it into a tangible goal takes guts! Just Do It.

Scoring yourself as you work toward your goal is a tremendous encouragement. I have a young high school friend, Ernie and Margaret Locklair's son, Richard, whose goal was to dunk a basketball by the end of his senior season. He could see himself doing it quite clearly. Though he didn't write it down, he shared his goal with a friend and talked about it constantly.

Player's Box

He scheduled a series of training exercises for himself, including buying a pair of strengthening shoes. Over time, his jump got noticeably higher. How could he tell? He scored himself regularly by jumping from the court to the basket with his fingers upheld. At first he could touch the rim with the first joint of his fingers. Then the second. One day he touched it with his palm. Although he did not reach his ultimate goal of dunking in a game, he did reap the benefits of a stronger jump, and one night scored a personal record of 26 points.

Because Richard didn't reach his goal by the end of his senior year, he has Set It Again. He knows he'll be invited to play in next year's Alumni Game. Now his goal is to dunk with the alums.

Setting new goals should be a lifelong process. Achieving a goal should be roundly and thoroughly celebrated, but it should not be a license to prop your feet on the coffee table and decompose once the work is done. Olympic athletes are often afflicted with this post-achievement malady. The great goal that has directed their lives for years is suddenly behind them. Soon — very soon — it will be time to set a new goal. It may be in an entirely different arena: education, perhaps, or business, or public service. Without it, life will simply be lived in the past.

To keep things in perspective before we move further:

(1) A Pro-Vision™ is a summary statement of your overall

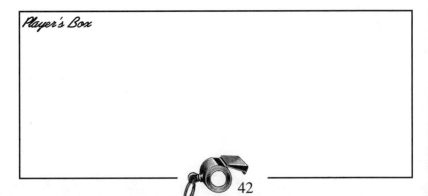

Player's Box

42

direction, either in your personal life or your business.

(2) Pro-Values™ are the personal attributes (such as integrity, courtesy, faith, creativity) that will govern your decisions and actions as you move in that direction.

(3) Goals are the specific actions you want to accomplish as part of your overall direction. Goals are essential if you're going to move forward, and not simply drift.

STUDYING THE CLIPS:

Lou Holtz, former football coach at the University of Notre Dame, is one of the most disciplined goal-setters and -achievers I've ever known. In the 1960's, he was hired as an assistant coach at the University of South Carolina by a head coach who resigned almost as soon as Holtz came on board. Paul Dietzel took USC's head coach's position, and after meeting with all the assistant coaches, told Holtz he didn't think he was going to make it as a collegiate coach.

Holtz went home to his wife, who was pregnant with their third child. They had just bought a new house with a sizeable mortgage. Lou Holtz sat down and wrote out 107 goals he wanted to accomplish in his lifetime. The list included such goals as milking a rattlesnake, flying off the deck of an aircraft carrier, and canoeing down the seven major rivers of the world. That's quite an extraordinary action for a person who's just

Player's Box

43

been fired.

One of the 107 goals included Holtz' desire to become head football coach at Notre Dame. He also wanted to win a national football championship. It has taken him over 20 years, but he has accomplished 99 of his original 107 goals. (We correspond periodically, and I keep track.) At Notre Dame, Holtz had every member of his team make out individual and team goals for the entire school year. The players carried them in their wallets wherever they went. The same was true for his assistant coaches.

The gymnast Mary Lou Retton is an example of someone who practiced the art of "seeing" her goals to perfection. Perhaps you were among the millions of viewers who watched her perform in the 1984 Olympics. If you studied her face before each gymnastic event, you could tell Retton was mentally performing every movement that was to come. Her head bobbed up and down as she "watched" herself take each running step to the vault. Years before, she had seen herself competing in the Olympics, and had set a goal: winning a gold medal. She had practiced these moves to perfection. Now, instead of paying attention to the crowd or the competition, she was able to see herself reaching her goal of performing each step perfectly, scoring a perfect 10 in each event before it took place. And that's what she did!

Since that time, it's become routine for Olympic athletes to

Player's Box

visualize themselves perfectly performing their events and routines. The 1996 Decathlon champion Dan O'Brien is a good example of this phenomenon. O'Brien's goal-setting and achieving is especially notable since he failed to even qualify in the 1992 Olympics.

Player's Box

STRETCHING EXERCISE:

Give serious thought to what you want to accomplish in your lifetime. Write down at least 10 goals. Remember to go through each of the Four S's. Write a date beside each goal to show when you want to see it realized.

TEAM STRETCHING EXERCISE:

Share some of the goals each member of the group has written down. Write on two 3x5 note cards at least three goals. Exchange one of the cards with another member of your group.

Follow up with your group member to see how he is doing on accomplishing his goals. Let him do the same for you.

FOCAL POINT:

"Go make yourself an ark of cypress wood; make rooms in it and coat it with pitch inside and out."   Genesis 6:14

Player's Box

Chapter 7
Life Is Not A Pie

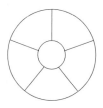

THE CHALK TALK:

The slice-size varies, and the labels change, but it's almost always a pie that's sketched when a speaker or author begins to describe the "pieces" of life and how each can be improved.

You've seen the charts. There's a slice for family life, a slice for your career, sometimes half a dozen or more slices which usually — not always — includes a slice for your spiritual life.

But there's an inherent fallacy in looking at life in such a way that the spiritual aspect is only a piece among pieces. You cannot relegate the soul to the status of just another piece, no matter whether it's a huge piece, an equal slice, or a sliver. I believe that unless the spiritual aspect is the center of your life, with all other parts radiating from that center, your life will eventually drain away through that empty center.

I call my diagram of life a Life Pre-Server™. If you mentally divide the ring into five segments, you'll note that each of those segments is radiating from the hole in the middle. It's a perfect picture of how God made us — with a hole in the very center of our being that cries out to be filled.

People have always known about the hole, which is why people have always worshipped a deity. Centuries ago the

Player's Box

French physicist, mathematician and philosopher Blaise Pascal observed, "There is a God-shaped vacuum in every man that only God can fill."

We know that nature (including human nature) abhors a vacuum and acts instantly to fill it. Some of us spend our entire lives trying to fill that inner vacuum within us. Our natural inclination is to fill it with anything other than God. But the soul is quite a monogamous creation. It has eyes only for the One who created it.

Lifesaver candy came into being in the early 1900's as a mistake. A candy-making machine malfunctioned, and the hard little disks came out with a hole in the middle. It wasn't until the 1990's that somebody realized the marketability of the tiny round centers, and started packaging them for sale, too. The hole in human beings, however, is no mistake, nor can it be filled by any of the same components in the outer ring. The God who made us also made the hole, and only He can satisfy its incessant longing to be filled. That's why no achieved goal will satisfy us completely, unless it's an achievement that fits within God's own goals as well. When it does, there is a sense of "rightness" and satisfaction that nothing can ever take away.

STUDYING THE CLIPS:

Before he was my friend, Scott Harrelson was my marketing student. Several years after graduation, Scott took a risk and

Player's Box

leased a Myrtle Beach, SC, building in which over nine previous restaurants had failed in an equal number of years. An inexperienced attorney conducted the trademark search on the name Scott first gave his restaurant, and he found himself being sued by a Northern company that owns a franchise by the same name.

Scott successfully negotiated for time to decide on the new name for his restaurant: Thoroughbreds. Meanwhile, he focused on creating an exceptional dining experience. Both food and decor were of highest quality. Entrees were given such names as Preakness and Kentucky Derby. Thoroughbreds was soon doing $2.5 million worth of business annually. Patrons gave it a "Best of the Beach" award, and in 1994, Scott was voted Entrepreneur of the Year by the South Carolina Restaurant Association. Scott was living exceptionally well by worldly standards, but I knew there was a hollowness in his life-style.

In 1996, I asked Scott where he was attending church. He replied, as many people do, that he was "just looking around." I invited him to our church, but told him I would pray that the Lord Himself would lead him to the place where He wanted him to worship. Scott showed up at our church within the month and became a regular. There is no altar call given in our church, but periodically, the minister explains the way of salvation, and invites those in the congregation to join him

Player's Box

silently as he prays a prayer of repentance and faith in Jesus Christ.

Scott told me later than he was tired of running his life his own way. He, the owner of Thoroughbreds, wanted an owner himself, besides himself. He said he prayed, asking Christ to become his savior and his Lord, and that he knew the transaction had taken place -- it was completely real to him. The hole inside had been filled, not with the square pegs of money or power or alcohol, but with the only One who truly fit. He turned what used to be a hole into "wholeness."

From a business standpoint, Scott was in high cotton, as we say in the South, but now the new center of his life was pointing him to serving Christ. This year Scott is focusing on what God would have him to do with his life. He is open to whatever direction the Lord leads.

Scott feels that he is moving from being merely successful to being significant, as *Halftime* author Bob Buford puts it. In satisfying the needs of his soul, Scott is also changing the way in which he conducts the other five areas of his life, which we look at in following chapters.

Player's Box

STRETCHING EXERCISE: Write down those things with which you have tried to fill the longing of your soul — both past and present. For each, ask yourself: did it truly satisfy me?

TEAM STRETCHING EXERCISE:

Discuss how the group members have tried to fill the "hole" in their lives. How long was it before emptiness set in again? What did you try next?

FOCAL POINT:

"In reply Jesus declared, 'I tell you the truth, unless a man is born again, he cannot see the kingdom of God.'" John 3:3

Player's Box

Chapter 8
The Body

THE CHALK TALK:

Do you have a perfect clone of your body hanging in your locker or your bedroom closet? When you get tired or sick, can you reach into the locker and pull out your new body, just like you'd pull out a fresh uniform?

It's highly unlikely! Unless researchers figure out how to let us trade bodies as readily as we trade houses, cars and computers, we're limited to the original model we were issued. Surgery can replace or repair parts, but only at a price.

God invented the most complex and remarkable machine in the world when he invented the human body. In case your faith in that fact has been shaken by computers that function like chess-masters, let's remember that each and every computer in the world, even the fastest and "smartest," is limited by the capabilities of the humans who built and programmed it.

GIGO is a computer term that means Garbage In, Garbage Out. That's a succinct way of saying that whatever you put into a computer determines the output. Your body is like a computer in that respect, too.

As with all machines, you have to feed it something. Computers want electricity and programs. Cars want gas, oil and

Player's Box

fluids. Your body wants food and drink.

As with all machines, you also have to invest time in preventive maintenance. No one operating an automobile is going to put water in the gas tank. The engine won't function. The preventive maintenance on a car is terrific — oil, filters, belts, fuses, fluids, tires — and that's just to protect its ability to function! If you also want it to look good, you've got to wash it, wax it, vacuum it, clean the upholstery, and keep up with any necessary body work and painting.

People take better care of computers and cars than we do of our bodies. I appreciate the old marketing slogan for Fram Oil Filters: "Pay me now or pay me later." Neglected bodies, especially if they're young, will run awhile without obvious breakdowns. It's the invisible degeneration going on inside that you eventually pay for. I think about the filters in our bodies — our kidneys, lungs and liver, for example. When they get dirty from cholesterol, smoke, alcohol, or drugs, there's no simple or painless way to pull out these filters and change them. I think about the system of hoses — the arteries and veins — that allows our body's "oil" to constantly circulate. When cholesterol buildup incapacitates a hose, we're talking doctors and hospitals, not a quick trip to the garage.

It's a great conundrum: we lavish care on countless man-made machines while we neglect the one magnificent machine that they're made to serve.

Player's Box

My mother, who's a certified antique dealer, will tell you that anything 50 years old and older is considered an antique. Well, my body is now a certified antique, but like one of those well cherished antique cars, it's still in excellent running condition. I'm deliberate about what I put into it, how much I put into it, and when I put it in! It wasn't always that way. How badly I damaged my kidneys and other body parts during the years that I was drinking, I don't know.

When it comes to the body, I've learned to operate on what I call the 4E Concept:
- eating
- exercise
- energy
- enjoyment

King Solomon said you can either eat to live or live to eat. I don't think he was trying to be funny. Some physicians estimate that 75 percent of Americans are overweight. It's not unusual for people to gain and lose over 500 pounds in their lifetime. Why? They fall into habits of unhealthy eating, and when they try to reverse the damage, never make the long-term life-style change that will allow them to keep the weight off. Basically, these people keep their old habits. They may go on a diet (notice that the first three letters spell "die") but dieters are only trying to temporarily kill their eating habits. Once the weight is off, they celebrate by eating the very foods they gave

Player's Box

up!

Once you make a commitment to changing, you can't go back to your old ways. You must make a permanent change both in attitude and eating habits — a life-style change. I've decided I will eat to live, but I won't be a slave to my appetite.

Neither can I be a slave to drink. Our bodies were made to run on water. Every single liquid we drink has water as its base, but we've figured out some tremendously unhealthy ways to jazz up a simple glass of H2O. The sugar content, the caffeine content, the alcohol content — all of this can make your drink detrimental to your health.

If you eat, you also must exercise. We have over 200 bones and 600 muscles in our body, and we need to exercise them on a regular basis — at least 30 minutes three to four times a week. I try to get in six exercise sessions a week if I possibly can. It's a habit I started at age 13 when I used the proceeds from a paper route to buy my first set of weights, and I've been lifting now for over 37 years. Walking, too, has become just as much of my daily routine as eating breakfast. It's another habit, something I build into my daily schedule. I write it down in my Daytimer. If someone calls and says, "What are you doing tomorrow at lunch?" and I've already blocked out lunch time for a workout, I answer truthfully, "I already have an appointment." It's an appointment with myself, an important one, that I may reschedule in an emergency but not on a whim.

Player's Box

What's the benefit? Energy! The energy you have right now comes from what you put into your body in food and drink over the last 36 to 48 hours. It takes that long for the food to be broken down and converted into usable energy. Today's meals will not have a marked impact on today's energy level, as long as you don't eat foods that make you sleepy or sluggish, such as red meat (hard to digest; pulls too much blood from your brain and muscles) or processed sugar (which gives you a false insulin high and then a huge crash afterwards.) So, if you have a big game or an important meeting on Friday, better pay attention to how you're eating long before Friday morning comes!

I want to enjoy my life! How I feel physically has such a tremendous bearing on my ability to live life fully and productively. Just as part of life's enjoyment is activity, its vital counterpart is rest. Getting enough sleep is simply a measure of establishing good habits, of saying "no" to a tempting activity. Another measure of health that doctors look for is a person's resting heart rate. Since a living heart never stops beating, it rests only between beats. Contradictory as it seems, proper exercise ensures that your heart will get the rest it needs. Boosting your heart rate during exercise produces a lower resting heart rate, because it strengthens the heart — a muscle that never stops flexing. Exercise also keeps the veins and arteries supple, which keeps the blood flowing freely to all

Player's Box

parts of the body.

A man's resting heart rate is typically about 70 heartbeats a minute; a woman's smaller heart averages 80. If you're a man, you want to get your resting heart rate into the mid-60's range or lower, and the mid-70's or lower for a woman. Marathon runners, most of whom are in great shape, sometimes have resting heart rates in the low 40's.

STUDYING THE CLIPS:

My early life was an excellent example of body-training gone awry.

I badly wanted to play high school football. I made the team in my junior year, but at 5'10" and 135 pounds, I was not what you would call all-star material. One night, we were involved in a close contest. It was late in the game and we had a chance of winning. One of our tackles got hurt. The coach shouted for a replacement. I just knew this was going to be my chance. I threw off my cape (not Batman style, but it *was* cold that evening) and rushed up to the coach. He took one look at me and shouted, "I mean a real player!" And with that he hit me with a forearm I'll never forget. The force of the blow knocked me across the bench. The next week, the coach put me off the team.

I thought my world had come to an end. When I could think again, I set a goal to make the varsity team my senior year. and

Player's Box

During the off-season, I ate a lot, lifted a lot of weights, and did a lot of running. By the time August of 1964 rolled around, I weighed a strong 145 pounds! I was ready to take on the world. And I made the squad! I had a wonderful senior year.

Dad was assigned to an Army post in Stuttgart, Germany, and I started college in Munich, at the University of Maryland's campus there. In Munich, I really got into lifting those Olympic weights. I had dreams of returning to the States and playing college football in the Southeastern Conference (SEC).

I had figured out that bigger was better where football was concerned, and it was in college that I violated my own training rules. Up to this point, I had a self-imposed rule — no drinking. No going into bars or parties where people were drinking, either. But I was really anxious to gain weight and build muscle. So I compromised. I started drinking beer on the weekends. I began picking up a few pounds, and soon I was drinking a couple of nights a week. Then it was every night.

By now I was up to 173 pounds, but I could bench press 325 and squat over 500. After writing to several schools, I received an encouraging letter from Coach Charlie Bradshaw at the University of Kentucky. He had lettered under Bear Bryant at UK in the early 50's as a 150-pound defensive end. Yes, Coach Bradshaw liked little players.

I transferred to UK in the fall of 1966. The second week into practice, the team doctor and team trainer called me over

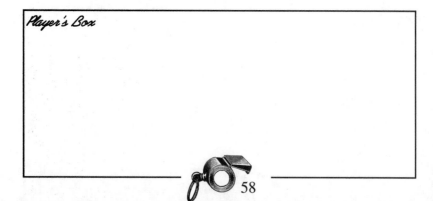

Player's Box

to discuss my running style. I had already had two ankle operations because of my polio. They suggested I consider a third operation to fuse the bones in my ankle.

If the operation worked, I would run faster than I ever had before. If it failed, I would be a real cripple the rest of my life. Now here was a risk I really had to weigh, and from a medical standpoint, I didn't feel the odds were on my side. I had some other goals in my life and they involved being able to walk.

As much as I loved football, I decided not to have the operation, and the coaches decided there were faster players who could take my place. Later, I became the freshman football dorm advisor, but I never put on another game uniform.

I didn't regret the choice I'd made about the surgery, but by now, I was definitely suffering the effects of my choice to drink.

When I became a Christian in 1975, I continued to drink — often. I wanted you to continue to be my friend, and if I didn't have what you drank, I'd go out and get it for you. In 1977, I was attending a church service and soon became convinced that although there were several hundred people in the sanctuary, the Lord was speaking directly to me. Bill Solomon, the man who led me to the Lord two years earlier, was preaching a sermon on I Corinthians 10:31: "So whether you eat or drink, or whatever you do, do it all for the glory of God."

At the end of the sermon, Bill held up a crumpled paper bag

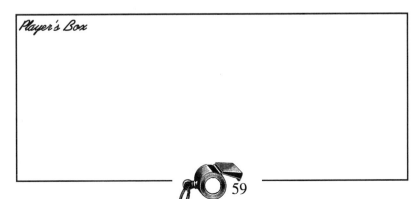

Player's Box

pulled out an empty beer can he'd found earlier that morning on the side of the road. He said, "The next time you go to drink a beer or other alcoholic beverage, raise it to the Lord first and praise Him with it. Then drink it!"

Have you ever had the wind knocked out of you? The Lord hit me right in the middle of the solar plexus. I must have had over $800 worth of liquor, wine and beer in the house (I always wanted to be prepared — besides, while living in Germany, I thought I had become a beer expert.) I knew I was not bringing glory to God in the way I drank alcohol. Now I wanted to get rid of it. First, I thought I'd sell it to my younger brothers. Then, I thought perhaps I'd just give it to them. And then I thought, "I better pour it all down the drain." That's just what I spent the rest of Sunday afternoon doing. The house smelled like a distillery!

That's the last time I ever had a drink. Though I'm not saying a Christian can never drink, I've found that God always calls us to give up those things that pose a danger to our own spiritual growth — or that of others. I Corinthians 10:31 became my personal mission statement, my Pro-Vision™.

Player's Box

STRETCHING EXERCISE:

Begin to conduct a series of two-day experiments. Choosing one at a time, eliminate certain foods and drinks from your daily diet. How do you feel without caffeine? Sweet drinks and snacks? Alcohol? Nicotine? If you find yourself shaking, whatever you gave up has likely become the center of your life. See what it is you're addicted to. Pray for the wisdom and strength to do what's best for your body. Set a goal and the date by which you want to accomplish it. Then get started.

Incidentally, there's a simple way to wean yourself off additives and back to water. Start with your evening meal. Substitute water for whatever you normally drink. Have several glassfuls. Expand your water-drinking to snack times and lunch. If you can't go cold turkey on caffeine, have one cup of coffee in the morning instead of two or three. Make it last a while. As soon as you get thirsty, drink some cold water. I know a 17-year-old athlete who loved cola drinks but realized they made him hyper. He talks now about how much "cleaner" and more energetic he feels since he's cut out all but very occasional sweets.

TEAM STRETCHING EXERCISE:

Discuss how you reacted to the two-day individual stretching exercise. How did you feel physically? Spiritually? Remember the discussion of habits from Chapter 5.

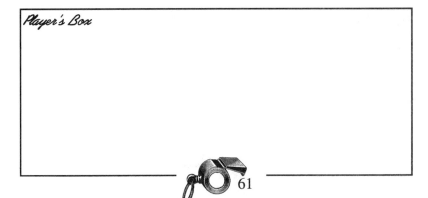

Player's Box

FOCAL POINT:

"No, I beat my body and make it my slave so that after I have preached to others, I myself will not be disqualified for the prize."   I Corinthians 9:22

Player's Box

Chapter 9
The Mind

THE CHALK TALK:

One of the best slogans ever created belongs to the United Negro College Fund. It raised both money and consciousness levels after national television ads launched it in the 1960's.

That slogan, "A mind is a terrible thing to waste," applies to every human being, not just those of color.

The Lord made your brain like a big CD. Physicians who conduct autopsies tell us that the brain becomes etched in the portions of gray matter that have been used for thinking. Where the gray matter is smooth, it has not been used. While we don't fully understand whether all gray matter is actually intended to be etched, scientists tell us that less than 10 percent of the average autopsied brain shows etching. That would indicate that we may have phenomenal untapped mental potential!

How are you using your mind?

• Actively or passively? Most television, for example, requires very little interaction. It's one thing to turn on the TV to learn, and quite another to vegetate in the name of amusement. But I don't buy the argument that it's always better to read a book than to watch television. Poorly chosen books are just as detrimental. It's commonplace to read for hours, put a

Player's Box

book down, and have nothing beneficial to show for it. The issue is selectivity. Being selective about television, movies and books shows that you respect the brain for its ability to absorb and apply. The GIGO analogy we discussed in the previous chapter relates just as strongly to the mind. Put garbage in and you will almost certainly find your brain producing thoughts of garbage — showing up in speech and actions when you least expect them. In most cases, selective reading will be more beneficial to you than selective viewing, because you are actively engaging your brain. You're actively reading, not just letting images pass in front of your eyes.

• Extraordinarily or mundanely? Some people have never learned the value of organizational tools, such as daily planners and personal telephone directories. It's a poor use of your mind to use it for remembering strings of numbers or lists of things to do. In fact, doing that can be stressful, since you may find yourself worrying that you'll forget things. Write things down, and carry the list with you. One of the world's most accomplished men, Thomas Jefferson, carried at all times a small fanlike notebook made of ivory. It was his daily habit to jot down observations of astonishing variety, on everything from philosophy to agriculture to meteorology to architecture. He transferred those notes into the appropriate record book each night, and erased the pencil marks from his ivory note-book — fresh to use the next day. This might be considered

Player's Box

the forerunner of the first laptop computer or electronic note-book. Relieving the mind of mundane record-keeping duties frees it for creative work.

• Creatively or uncreatively? Mike Vance, former dean of the Disney Institute, and Diane Deacon, president of the Creative Thinking Association, added a phrase to the world's languages when they published their book, *Think Out of the Box*. Their prologue includes a graphic of a box created from nine dots, with the challenge to connect those dots with straight lines, without raising your pencil from the paper. The solution is maddeningly simple once you realize that your lines have to extend outside the box formed by the dots. Creative thinking is like that, too. We have to push our minds past the familiar and comfortable and into the exciting places where minds can grow.

Suppose you operate a restaurant, and you're working to define what makes your restaurant distinctive. In other words, you want to put together a Pro-Vision™ statement. You may assume you're in the food business, but by thinking creatively, you realize you're in the atmosphere business. That's what people pay for — whether they're going to a fast-food establishment for a quick pit stop (note that the booths are hard and the music lively, to encourage you to eat faster and free up the seat for the next customer) or enjoying an evening of dining excellence at a fine restaurant, with its padded chairs, its soft slow music, and its expectation that you'll spend at least two

Player's Box

hours at your table. Plus there's the middle niche — the family restaurant or the theme restaurant. Regardless, it's all atmosphere. The more creatively thinking restauranteurs are looking at their patrons and their business and deciding how they can create a distinction in dining. Likewise, a clothier is not simply in the clothes business, but in the image business. A public relations agent is in the persuasion business. You must think outside the obvious, outside the ordinary, to be a pro. It goes without saying that you must always think in terms of excellence.

• Applying or failing to apply? Unless you simply enjoy impressing people with facts (and they probably won't appreciate it), knowledge is no good to you unless you apply it. Many people have bought the idea that "knowledge is power," but that's an erroneous concept. It is the USE of knowledge that is power. Suppose you've elevated your reading standards and find a book that truly does contain lessons that can improve your life. Will you take the steps to implement them? Will you apply what you've learned? To simply accumulate knowledge leaves you a giant step short of acquiring wisdom, which comes with doing what you know is right. This is a principle most easily seen in the way we read the Bible, the best playbook in the world. In fact, it is the world's best selling book, though some say it is also the world's least read book. The apostle James wrote that "Faith without works is dead."

Player's Box

Likewise, the Bible tells us that if we know what is right to do, but do not do it, that lack of action is sin. There are people who fully understand that God is calling them to Himself. They understand that He requires them to repent of sin. They understand that Jesus took the punishment for their sin by dying in their place. But they never step over the line. They may call themselves Christians, but they are actually fooling themselves, like those people who buy a membership at a gym, and seem to feel that they are physically fit just from walking in and watching others sweat. We really do reap what we sow.

STUDYING THE CLIPS:

Back in the spring semester of 1988, I had an unusually high number of potential entrepreneurs in my retailing class at Coastal Carolina University. Three international students particularly stood out.

As always, there was a project involved in my class. Working in teams, each pair of students was given the same assignment: to design a retail operation in nearby Myrtle Beach. Each had to develop an entire turnkey operation through a written business plan — the marketing, financial statements, staff training, store layout — eight segments in all. It was demanding, and stopped short only at actually opening the business.

Player's Box

In the spring of 1988, two Icelandic students (the soccer coach frequently recruited from Iceland) came to me after the first week of class and told me they did not want to design a business in Myrtle Beach.

No, Karl and Gunnar wanted to open an actual home delivery pizza business in Reykjavic, their nation's capital. At the time, there was not a single such business in all of Iceland. You could go to a pizza parlor to place an order, but there was no home delivery.

I didn't know a thing about the business climate of Iceland, and frankly, the idea of designing and actually opening a business 3,000 miles away seemed a bit hopeless. It was far easier for me to monitor the development of a hypothetical business in my own backyard. It would have been all too simple to rattle off a list of potential problems and require the boys to stick to the original assignment.

But I believed in the principles I was teaching, and by now, I had also learned to seize an opportunity, since all too often, the right time never comes again. I agreed that Karl and Gunnar could tackle their project — never dreaming what would take place. For two months, from mid-January until spring break in mid-March, they really worked. Gunnar flew home to Iceland during break to present to a bank the financial statements he and Karl had developed. The banker actually gave them a loan!

By the summer, a business known as Jon Bakken (translated

Player's Box

Johnny's Bread — there is no Icelandic word for pizza) was in operation in downtown Reykjavic. By the time my two students graduated from Coastal, they had a thriving pizza delivery business operating in four locations. Karl went back to Iceland to run the business. Gunnar went on to get a master's degree in international business from the top-ranked program at the University of South Carolina.

By 1993, Coastal Carolina University had over 20 Icelandic business graduates. That spring, I received a call from one of them. Dolli explained that he and a number of others had taken all my marketing classes, had my books and notes, but didn't have me.

He wanted to know if I would consider coming to Reykjavic to conduct a series of marketing seminars for their various businesses. I told him I would be delighted. So during spring break, I flew to Iceland for 10 days. During that time, I got to sample the best pizza I had ever tasted in my life — Jon Bakken! What began as a dream in a retailing class 3,000 miles away and five years earlier was now an established business — with 100 employees in five locations selling 15,000 pizzas a month. In 1997 the two entrepreneurs sold Jon Bakken for a new direction in their lives.

In that same 1988 class was a varsity tennis player named Ash from India. As their class project, he and a classmate, Sanjay, developed a plan to open an Indian restaurant, getting

Player's Box

up at 5 a.m. on the day of their presentation to cook a delicious chicken curry for the entire class. It wasn't a restaurant that Ash actually opened after graduation, however. Today, he and his partners own five convenience stores in Raleigh, NC, each of which grosses over $1 million.

Player's Box

STRETCHING EXERCISE:

Think about something that you have been putting off that requires the use of "mind power." Perhaps it is reading a special book, watching an instructional video, taking a course to improve yourself. (Maybe it is to go back and actually start the Stretching Exercises at the end of each of the previous chapters.) Whatever it is, start it now!

TEAM STRETCHING EXERCISE:

Recommend quality books, videos and courses to the other members of your group. What makes them worthwhile? How have they affected your thinking?

FOCAL POINT:

"Finally brothers, whatever is true, whatever is noble, whatever is right, whatever is pure, whatever is lovely, whatever is admirable, if anything is excellent or praiseworthy, think about such things." Philippians 4:8

Player's Box

Chapter 10
Love

THE CHALK TALK:

No doubt about it. Allowing yourself to love makes you vulnerable to loss, to rejection, to being misunderstood. You can bring home a head-swelling salary and shoot better golf than a Master's contender, but, unless you love, there's a hollow rattle where your pounding heart should be.

Love is fundamental to life. Without it, we become pitiable. At worst, we become evil. And in some cases, it's been demonstrated that we die without it. Strange, then, that love is such a hard word for men and women to get a handle on.

We grasp it in pieces. In thinking about love, men often think first of sexual intimacy. Many women, on the other hand, think of love as emotional intimacy. Both kinds of intimacy are genuine parts of love.

But parts only. When a man offers emotional intimacy as a means of getting sex, or when a woman approaches sex as a means of gaining emotional intimacy, the hollow rattling soon begins all over again. The emptiness remains. Men and women were created to experience a greater kind of love.

Probably the most widely memorized Bible verse worldwide is John 3:16. "For God so loved the world," the verse

Player's Box

declares, "that He gave his only begotten Son, that whosoever believeth on Him should not perish but have everlasting life." Look closely at the first nine words: "For God so loved the world that He gave..."

This is the highest summary of love ever modeled, a love based on costly giving, not getting. Despite that fact, it is the most satisfying brand of love in existence.

It's the most versatile, as well. It applies to parents, children, friends, neighbors, co-workers and perfect strangers, as well as to spouses.

For the purposes of explaining this slice of your Life Preserver™, we're focusing on the circle of people you are closest to: those you live with, and those blood relatives who belong in the innermost circle of those you love best.

When there is happiness between you and the members of your inner circle, you have distinct advantages in life. You know you are not alone. There are people you can count on. There are people who will drop everything to come to you in a crisis.

But if ongoing tension marks your closest relationships, that tension will eventually show up to the detriment of your job, your health, virtually every facet of life, right down to your golf game. Our closest relationships define us.

Relationships of all kinds take time and work but especially those with the people we're closest to. It's been said, for ex

Player's Box

ample, that children spell love T-I-M-E. (That means focused, one-on-one time, not merely time spent in the same house.) To spend time with someone is to give. Time is precious to us, and to give it is costly.

The fact is, relationships of all kinds involve giving, giving, giving. We have to give time and we have to give effort. We have to consciously give love, even when we don't particularly want to. And we have to consciously give forgiveness, especially when we don't want to. Quality relationships take a pro-active, Pro-Vision™ kind of love, and they take a tremendous amount of forgiveness.

Dr. Gary Chapman broke important ground in his 1992 book, *The Five Love Languages*, put out by Northfield Publishing. Chapman, a professional marriage counselor, believes there are basically five languages people use to express and receive love. The five include:

- words of affirmation
- acts of service
- gifts
- quality time
- physical touch.

Chapman contends that each of us uses one of these five as our primary love language, but that people seldom marry someone who speaks the same language. For example, a man whose primary language is "gifts" may feel most loved when

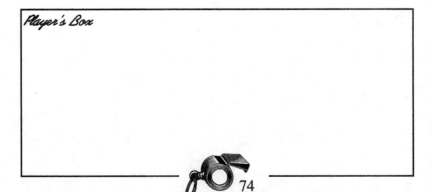

Player's Box

his wife notices the tool he's been studying in a mail order catalog, buys it and presents it to him. He may try to express his love to her in the same way, but wonders why she seldom seems to respond to the earrings or the lingerie he buys. She, however, speaks the language of "acts of service." For now, she would feel far more loved by his decision to help her paint the bedroom than by his presentation of a pair of diamond earrings.

Chapman says that within each of the five languages (and note that each of these five requires giving, whether of words, service, gifts, time or touch) there are an unlimited number of "dialects."

For example, my writing partner, Margaret Locklair, shouldn't have been surprised to realize that her love language is "words of affirmation." But the specific kind of words, the dialect, came as a surprise. Margaret had reluctantly agreed to take snow skiing lessons, under pressure from her family and friends. Struggling to keep both legs in the same general plane, she finally succeeded in following her instructor's snowplowing directions. The instructor unleashed a torrent of encouragement: "Great job! That's the way to do it! You're really getting it." He gave another command, and Margaret found herself trying harder this time. When he encouraged her the third time, she was shocked to realize there were tears in her eyes. "His words of encouragement affected me to the

Player's Box

point," she said later, "that if he'd told me to ski off the side of the mountain, I think I would have done it."

Suddenly, she had tremendous insight into herself: Why, for example, she found it hard to work for editors who gave her little feedback, either positive or negative; why she felt cut off from a loved one who once complained she was always "flattering" him. Now, Margaret realized, he spoke a different language, and what she had meant as encouragement for trying, he had interpreted as empty flattery.

It takes work to learn someone else's language, it's an all-too-common human failing to take for granted those we feel we no longer have to impress. As soon as we gain a sense of security in a relationship, we tend to slip out of our "courtship manners" and back into our old skin, saying, "If you love me, you'll overlook my faults. I've always had these faults, and I don't intend to give them up. I'm uncomfortable speaking your language, and you're just going to have to learn mine."

But in doing that, we stop growing, and so do the people in our closest circle. People who love each other have a responsibility not to look the other way, but to give, helping one another conquer the faults that lead to atrophy and eventually death. And it must be done in love.

Pursue love actively — not just the conquest phase of love, but the uphill challenge of staying in love. And practice forgiveness. These are two examples perfectly set for us by God,

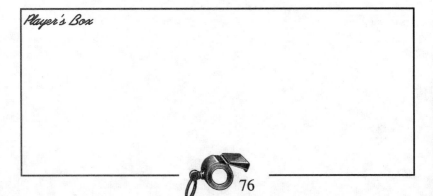

Player's Box

and they apply to every human relationship.

STUDYING THE CLIPS:

By the time we found out that my father-in-law Art had lung cancer, it was too late to do much more than keep him comfortable. My wife and I brought him home with us, and for the next month, I watched him battle to breathe, day by day, hour by hour, minute by minute, and second by second. Despite the fact that he had been quite an athlete in his younger days (a Golden Gloves Boxer and a high school football player) he had chosen to smoke. After all, he may have reasoned as a teenager, he had his whole life ahead of him. Why worry about a few puffs a day? Now, in his last days of life, he was bringing up long strings of white phlegm that looked like glue. Soon, his throat closed up to the point that he ate nothing, and every day, we watched his body shrink in front of our eyes. The effects of making that smoking choice was taking its deadly toll.

Despite the fact that Zoe Ann and I had been married 26 years, have four children and a stable home life, there was a barrier that stood between Art and me. It was an old wall, erected the day Zoe Ann and I eloped. Now, despite the fact that we had enjoyed a good relationship in recent years, I knew that I could not effectively take care of Art as long as the wall stood.

Player's Box

One morning, just after he came to stay with us, I went into Art's bedroom to ask if there were anything I could do to make him more comfortable or if there were anything I could get for him. He said in his dry, witty way, that he'd like to have his health. Then he asked me how much longer I thought he might hang on. I told him I didn't know, that only the Lord knew, and he said with a big smile, "And He ain't talking today."

Art had always been a very direct person. He told you exactly how he felt and what he thought about things. That had often caused conflict between the two of us. We had strong differences of opinion about practically everything. Over the years, to keep peace in the house, I had learned not to disagree with him openly when he visited us. That made him mad, too.

Now, sitting by his bedside, I worked up my courage and decided to give. I asked Art to forgive me for not being the son-in-law he had always wanted. He looked at me for a long time with his piercing eyes. His mind was still sharp, but he had difficulty responding now that the cancer was spreading so quickly. He said, "I forgive you, and will you forgive me?" I said, "Yes." And he said, "Let's speak of it no more."

I was amazed at how quickly this transaction had taken place, and at how profound a difference it would make in our relationship over the next few weeks. For most of my life, when I had done something wrong, I would say, "I'm sorry," sometimes meaning it, and sometimes not. For the first time in

Player's Box

my life, I recognized the power of asking someone to forgive me, rather than saying merely, "I'm sorry." And that made all the difference in my relationship with Art and my family through the remaining weeks of his life. I would not trade that conversation for anything. It was one of the most powerful lessons on relationships I have ever learned and it took a dying man to teach it to me.

Now I ask myself why I waited so long to ask Art's forgiveness. Pride, I suppose, but maintaining that pride cost me the freedom to forge a relationship with a man who could have been a source of much wisdom and counsel for me.

Player's Box

STRETCHING EXERCISE ONE:

Sit down with the person you're closest to and ask Dr. Chapman's favorite question: "Will you write down three or four things I could do to make you feel loved? Please be extremely specific." Look at the answers carefully. Do you see a pattern? Is there a specific love language evident, or do you need to ask probing questions to find it? Realizing that you may feel uncomfortable speaking that language, resolve to do it anyway, at least once a day. It may take a few weeks to see results because your partner may not trust you to keep it up. Remember, you are giving. The getting will come in its own time.

STRETCHING EXERCISE TWO:

Read God's description of love in I Corinthians 13. The entire chapter is known as the "Love Chapter," but verses 4 through 8 are particularly pointed. They say, "Love is patient, love is kind. It does not envy, it does not boast, it is not proud. It is not rude, it is not self-seeking, it is not easily angered, it keeps no record of wrongs. Love does not delight in evil, but rejoices with the truth. It always protects, always trusts, always hopes, always perseveres." Can you truthfully put your name in the place of each "love" or "it"?

Player's Box

STRETCHING EXERCISE THREE:

Life is too short to tell someone that you love him or her only at Christmas time or Mother's Day or a birthday. If you have never said, "I love you" to someone you really love, do it now! That person may not be there when you're finally ready to say it. Don't wait.

TEAM STRETCHING EXERCISE ONE:

Have each group member think of a time when a loved one seemed to respond with unusual enthusiasm or gratitude to something you did. Discuss how you can do more of that kind of giving.

TEAM STRETCHING EXERCISE TWO:

What areas of 1 Corinthians 13: 1-8 does each group member find most difficult to live out? Why?

FOCAL POINT:

"And now these three remain: faith, hope and love. But the greatest of these is love." I Corinthians 13: 13

Player's Box

Chapter 11
Peers

THE CHALK TALK:

Acquaintance-making, for most of us, is so constant we hardly recognize the process. Some acquaintances work and play beside you, contributing to a common goal. Some will stress you, stretch you, and challenge you to explore. From most, you will eventually separate or simply drift away. A few will become genuine friends.

The question is: of your hundreds of acquaintances, how will you decide which of them has the makings of a genuine friend?

I don't have a huge number of friends. Neither, apparently, did Henry Brooks Adams, who wrote, "One friend in a lifetime is much; two are many; three are hardly possible." To me, a friend is someone you would die for, literally. He and I have the same values. A true friend is someone I can call at 3:00 in the morning, and say, "Look, I've got to have $5,000 by tomorrow morning," and he would say, without a question, "Okay, where do you want me to deliver it?" A true friend and I are a club unto ourselves.

I do have a tremendous number of acquaintances. I may try to get to know someone because I like what I've heard him say,

Player's Box

or what I think he stands for. Likewise, the other person may be "friendly" toward me in the same, exploratory kind of way. Or one of us may want to cultivate an acquaintance to convince the other to buy into whatever we're selling. There's nothing wrong with that, as long as both of us understand our motives up front.

But how do you know which acquaintances and potential friends to cultivate? And once established, how do you help the relationship grow?

Roy Disney once said that when you know your values as a company, you won't have any trouble making corporate decisions. The same concept applies to personal friendships. When you know your personal values (see chapter 3), it's simple to ask yourself, "Does this person have basically the same values and goals I have? Will he boost me toward my goals, or will he pull me away?" It is vitally important that you know your own values.

If you're going out with a group, for example, and someone pulls out the latest recreational drug, and the bag comes to you, that's the wrong time to determine your values about drug usage. The peer pressure is going to be overwhelming because you know that if you don't take part, the group will not trust you. And if you do, you've bought into their value system whether you wanted to or not. They trust you. You're part of their "club." By association, when you join a particular club,

Player's Box

you're embracing the values the club stands for. Other people will now associate those same values with you.

Before you're willing to call someone a friend, ask yourself: can I, in good conscience, support this person's goals ... values ... lifestyle? Am I willing to be this person's encourager? Am I willing to be confrontational when he or she veers off course? Will I work to get him or her back on track? Am I willing to be inconvenienced for this person? All of these are solid, Biblical bases for choosing a friend.

Secondly, once you've established a friendship, how do you keep the relationship alive? We all enjoy spontaneity, but life has a way of crowding out people we don't see or hear from regularly. We become absorbed in our nuclear families, our jobs, our own circles, and people who were once close to us become "used-to-knows." Continental drift is insignificant compared with the drifting that takes place between people too busy to keep a relationship going.

Just like a good marriage, a good friendship takes effort and planning. Books on building a better business are filled with tips on how to relate to people. Many of those same tips apply to building personal relationships. Since I enjoy experimenting with different business concepts, I regularly apply those that seem sound. Some work for me and others don't. Here are a few of the ones that do:

I'm a business card collector, and I also hand them out

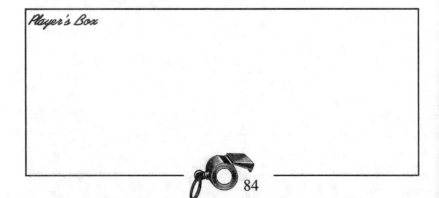

Player's Box

liberally. A fresh order of 1,500 cards usually lasts me about nine months. To an auto or real estate sales person, that's not a huge number, but in my business, it's plenty. That means I'm giving out well over 150 cards a month — an average of seven cards a day, based on a 20-day business month. I bring home an average of five cards per working day. When I get home, I review the day by pulling out the cards. On the back of each, I record any facts to remember about the person who gave me the card. I store the cards in vinyl business card files, some organized by geographical location, some by profession, and some in a separate file for my former students.

I review my business card files regularly, probably twice a month. Whenever the folder gets too thick, I cull out the business people I haven't been in contact with and feel I probably won't pursue an acquaintance with.

For each friend and client, I make an index card and periodically update it with important information such as a promotion, a birth in the family, names of family members, the person's birthday and anniversary.

I carry note paper, pens, and stamps in the car, which is like my second office. I use them daily to write brief notes to people to let them know I'm thinking of them. Birthdays, anniversaries and holidays are standard times to do this, but I try to write at other times of the year as well. When I read a news article involving someone I know, I'll frequently dash off a note to him congratulating him on his promotion or whatever earned his recognition.

When someone writes me a note or a letter, I try to write back within 10 days. I know that if the letter sits unanswered for any period of time, I will forget.

E-mail is a great way to stay in touch, and if the recipient reads it immediately, he can respond within minutes. I generally write and send E-mail at night.

I'm more of a writer than I am a caller; writing is less intrusive on the schedule of a busy person but, occasionally, I'll call just to say hello.

It may have been my grandfather who instilled the love of note-writing in me. I didn't get to see him very often when I was growing up because the Army kept my family moving. But we wrote to each other often. In the fall of 1962, my family had just moved from Southern California to South Carolina. Just after the presidential elections, my grandfather wrote me a letter, put a four-cent stamp on it, and folded a five dollar bill inside for my brothers and me to get ice cream. He sealed the letter, walked to the mailbox, walked back home, and dropped dead of a heart attack at age 65. Two days later, knowing that he was dead, I got his surprise in the mailbox. That was the strangest feeling of my life, knowing that I owed my grandfather a letter and that I would never be able to write him back. Obviously, I cherished that letter. The five dollars is still in the

Player's Box

original envelope. I still pull out the letter and read it and feel tangibly connected to a man who loved me.

If you want to communicate something complex, letters are better than a phone call. The penning or typing of a letter takes more time and thought. You can choose your words carefully and for maximum impact. You won't have to worry about voice inflections or awkward pauses in conversation, or being interrupted before you've finished what you want to say. And your letter can be saved and reread, digested at length.

Even when the subject matter isn't deep—just a "hi, how are you?" — note may be the encouragement that a friend needs on a particular day. Don't make your entire letter a recital of what's been going on in your life. At least once in every note, ask a specific question that gives the person a reason to call or write back. Let him know you're interested in him as a person. Most communication is surface; yours shouldn't be.

STUDYING THE CLIPS:

Len Bias was a fine college basketball player at the University of Maryland in the mid-1980's. After his senior year, he signed a multimillion dollar contract to play for the Boston Celtics.

You'll never read any statistics on Mr. Bias in the Celtic record books, however. Len's best friend suggested they cel

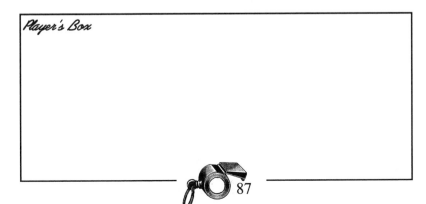

Player's Box

ebrate his contract with some cocaine. Len overdosed and died on June 17, 1986.

Today, there is only a small marker identifying the grave of a young man who could have been nationally celebrated. Your peers' values can quickly become yours. That's why having a written Pro-Vision™ and Pro-Value™ statement will help you choose your friends and the people you really want to be associated with.

Consider a radically different type of peer relationship.

Andrew Provence was an outstanding high school football player who followed his older brother Jerome on a football scholarship to the University of South Carolina. There, Andrew was named an All-American defensive player. He was a good student, too. It looked like he could have anything he wanted until he met Angie.

Angie liked Andrew, but as a Christian, she had made a decision that she would marry only another Christian, and she told him that. For Andrew, it was a major decision. He had the "head knowledge" about Christ without actually knowing Him personally. He had never put Christ first in his life.

Over a period of months, as he observed Angie's consistent character and that of her friends, Andrew decided he needed Christ, whether he ever married Angie or not. He gained both. Andrew went on to play professionally for the Atlanta Falcons and the Denver Broncos.The father of seven children,

Player's Box

he now has a Christian ministry to business people. Life can be so rewarding when you choose your friends and associates wisely.

Friends, especially Christian friends, know that they can reach out (sometimes over 11 time zones) when they're in need. I met Kalimash Khudzhimiratova in May of 1992 when she served as an interpreter on a Campus Crusade for Christ mission in her native Kazakhstan, a former Russian province. While we were there, Kalimash became a Christian. For three years, I prayed that she might be able to visit America, and through God's providence, she celebrated the Fourth of July with our family in 1995.

Since that time, things have gone from bad to worse in the former Soviet Republic. In the winter of 1996, there was no electricity in Kalimash's city. That included her apartment, which Kalimash had purchased for $3,000 by making a down payment of $1,500, with the balance to be paid in 1997. But because the government had gone broke, she had no income and was about to lose the apartment. Though it is extremely difficult to get letters in and out of Kazakhstan, the Lord enabled her letter to reach us, and simultaneously, provided the money for us to help her. No, the money didn't have her name written all over it, and yes, we could have kept the money and used it for ourselves. But the timing of the arrival of both her letter and the money convinced Zoe Ann and me that this

Player's Box

was the way God was responding to the needs of another believer, and we were excited to think that He was willing to trust us to carry out His plans.

STRETCHING EXERCISE ONE:

Write down the names of all of your true friends. Think about what you have in common with each one, and write it down. Recall the last time you communicated with them. Begin today to set a timetable to get in touch with each one of them.

STRETCHING EXERCISE TWO:

Decide how you want to keep track of people you meet, whether through business cards, index cards, file folders, computerized notebook or an e-mail address file. Begin setting up a system for yourself.

TEAM STRETCHING EXERCISE ONE:

Discuss how the group members handled the exercise involving true friends. Why does it appear to be so difficult for men to have real friends, based on nothing other than friendship?

TEAM STRETCHING EXERCISE TWO:

May I recommend Harvey Mackay's latest book, *Dig Your Well Before You Are Thirsty*? See how the group responds to it.

FOCAL POINT:

"Bad company corrupts good character."
I Corinthians 15:38

Player's Box

Chapter 12
Work

THE CHALK TALK:

Did you choose your profession or fall into it, like a pit?

Did you enter a particular field because a relative did the same work, or a friend had contacts, or the job seemed glamorous, or it offered security? As long as you're well-suited for it, all of those can be valid springboards for entering a profession. If not, they can be terribly invalid, and you can be missing a tremendous and exhilarating sense of fulfillment.

To every person on the face of the earth, God has given specific talents, as well as a built-in drive to develop and use them. The greatest degree of work-related satisfaction, the highest level of self-investment, comes from pursuing and using the talents in your personal "portfolio."

Tragic, then, that so many people lock themselves into jobs they really don't like. They invest years in a career that requires them to put on a mask every morning, assuming that over time, they'll grow to like this pit. After all, other people seem to like it. The money is decent. Over time, however, the sense of having made a wrong choice either paralyzes you or makes you bitter. Soon, you're telling yourself you have only ten more years until retirement. You live on a shaky sense of security that

Player's Box

the company will take care of you. Instead of living life now and enjoying it, you postpone the pleasure, living for the day you can retire. How often you hear people say, "When I retire, I'm going to do what I want to do." Ironic, isn't it, that so many men drop dead within six months after retirement?

Look at the math of it. If you put into a job the typical eight hours a day, five days a week, and you work 50 weeks a year, that's 2,000 hours a year. Multiply 2,000 hours a year by 40 years and that's 800,000 hours that you'll spend in a typical working career. That's a lot of hours to hate what you do. Why not — what a radical thought! — Enjoy them?

If your Pro-Vision™ is accurate and your Pro-Values™ are true, they will lead you to the work that you can do best — and enjoy. Even so, chances are strong that you'll change careers, but when you're working *with* instead of *against* your talents, each new job builds on the last. I have known since I was probably 10 or 12 that I'm a good leader, that I love to teach and instruct. I love working in situations where people pull together for a common goal or cause. But my perception of how to use those talents centered around being a public school teacher, and I wanted to make money! I changed majors four times in college, and wound up with a degree that would allow me to teach chemistry, but I never used it. Instead I went into coaching, which I loved. Eventually, I found myself teaching business on a college level while working with a coaching staff,

Player's Box

and I really loved that. Then, the Lord turned me from teaching on a college level to teaching within corporations (a form of coaching in itself), while also coaching youth league teams in the afternoons. Now I have the best of spiritual and secular pursuits, wrapped into one life. I am doing the things I do best, the things I love. Working in situations where people are pulling together for a common goal or cause applies both to business and sports. From a worldly perspective, I have no job security, but I know that I have the Lord, and that he will provide work for me. It's a wonderful life!

How do you ensure that you will find a job you will love? You have to go back to your Pro-Vision™ and your Pro-Values™ and begin to examine the way you're living. Ask yourself, "If I could do anything in the world of work, what would it be?" Then begin listing everything that's keeping you from doing it. Seriously look at what you can do to overcome those obstacles and align yourself to do this type of work. Ask yourself if the Lord has really given you the talents required to be excellent in that field. And then, once and for all, make up your mind to do one of two things: either turn all of your energies to accomplishing that life's work, or quit complaining.

If you're in a job you really can't afford to leave, you have to mentally make an attitude adjustment. You have to accept the fact that you may have been placed here for a reason beyond your understanding. Rather than hate and gripe about what you

Player's Box

do, you've got to reposition yourself to find even small joys in being gainfully employed versus being in the unemployment line — or dead.

This will make a tremendous difference: " Work as unto the Lord, and not as if unto men." That should apply to every job, but it becomes very meaningful to a man working in the pit. Don't work solely to impress a human boss so that you'll get a promotion or a raise, but work with the mental image of the Lord as your boss. Once you've grasped what He's already done for you, it's much easier to do less-than-fascinating work with a sincere and industrious attitude. Consciously change your attitude. Everyone knows the wonderful example of the glass of water: do you see it half-full or half empty? One is a positive outlook, and one is negative. How will you look at your work?

A word of warning: when you do align your work with your innate talents, it's so easy to find your greatest identity in your work. It's so easy to let work become your focus, to let it take over the center hole of the Life Pre-Server™ and become your god. When that happens, your life will shift out of balance. Every decision you make — what you eat or wear or read, how much time you spend with your family, who your friends are -- will all be predicated on how that decision affects your work. Life can be in balance only when God is your center. Every part of life — the physical, the mental, the

Player's Box

95

intimate, the peers and yes, the work — must radiate from a spiritual center where God inhabits His rightful place, in order for your life to be in balance.

STUDYING THE CLIPS:

Sometimes circumstances seem to divert us from the career of our choice. But I believe that God gives us opportunities to work in fields where we can use our God-given talents. It seems to be one of those general blessings that falls like sunshine and rain on believers and unbelievers alike.

Consider Jacques Cousteau. As a young boy, he was always fascinated with the sea. He made plans to become a naval pilot, but a very serious auto accident left him unable to pass the flight physical. To strengthen his arms, he took up swimming, then diving. Eventually, instead of becoming an aviator of the air, he became the world's premiere pilot of the sea. The Lord allowed him to take a tragedy, the loss of something he had wanted to do since he was a young man, and turn it into his all-consuming life's work. History is full of such examples.

Let's look at two American examples: the young Bobby Richardson from Sumter, SC, and the young Michael Jordan from Wilmington, NC. When Bobby was in the ninth grade, he was cut from his high school baseball team by a coach who

Player's Box

said he lacked the ability to play. When Michael was in the tenth grade, he was cut from his high school basketball team for the same reason.

Neither of these young men allowed this setback to keep them from pursuing their dream, their joy, their focus in life. Bobby Richardson was scouted the very summer after being cut, while playing American Legion ball. Both went on to have outstanding professional careers in their sport; Bobby as a record-setting second baseman for the New York Yankees, Michael as an All-Star for the Chicago Bulls.

Isn't it interesting that someone as athletically talented as Michael Jordan still has to stay within the lines of a basketball court to find true joy in his profession? You may remember that he had the briefest of careers as a minor league baseball player in 1995, but quickly discovered that, while he was good, he wasn't good enough to play on the level of his own expectations. Nevertheless, he was willing to take a chance on a new career. I admired the risk he took physically — if he had gotten hurt, he might never have been able to return to basketball. And I admire his willingness to live the less-than-exalted life of a minor league ballplayer, riding the bus and eating fast food like everybody else. What I really admired, however, was the statement he made to the effect that there was no shame in failure, only in not trying.

Jordan found out that his greatest professional satisfaction

Player's Box

would come in using the talent he was given, the talent he had developed to the peak of physical and mental prowess. Your great talent may not be athletic, but whatever it is, it holds the key to tremendous joy and satisfaction.

Player's Box

STRETCHING EXERCISES:

Review both your Pro-Vision™ and Pro-Values™ to see if they truly reflect the God-given talents you believe you have. Ask yourself, "Am I really happy - no, joyful - about the work that I do?" Begin now thinking about the changes you can make either in attitude or in your job itself to make your life more fulfilling. Don't wait. Especially don't wait until you retire. It may be too late then!

TEAM STRETCHING EXERCISE:

Discuss the dangers of finding your primary identity in your work. How can you keep your work in its proper place? If possible, bring in information from reputable career counselors.

FOCAL POINT:

"Whatever you do, work at it with all your heart, as working for the Lord, not for men."   Colossians 3:23

Player's Box

Chapter 13
Time

THE CHALK TALK:

Some sports, such as soccer, are slavish about time. They simply start the clock and let it run. When time runs out, the game is over. Other sports, like baseball, treat time more casually, measuring it in outs and innings, not minutes. And some sports virtually ignore time. Golf, for example, can be played at a snail's pace, with breaks for conversation and drinks.

People's attitudes toward time usually fall into these same categories.

Some people strap on their watches as soon as their feet hit the floor. They check their watches throughout the day, constantly monitoring time's passage. Others actually seem allergic to clocks. Watches make their skin crawl, and they operate on an internal "body clock" that tells them, not always reliably, when it's time to move on to the next activity. Others of us live in the middle, referring to the time periodically without feeling owned by it.

Both extremes and everyone in between can benefit from recognizing time as humanity's greatest "natural" resource, and managing it. Some will manage it loosely, making ample provision for serendipity. Others will manage it as aggressively

Player's Box

as we do wetlands and air quality.

But the point is, time should be managed. Time is a great equalizer. Everybody from richest to poorest has the same amount of it: 84,600 seconds per day. No one can truly buy any more. Some people just use what they have better than others.

If you're serious about managing your time, it is vital to consult your list of goals and map out where you're heading in the time you have.

Those readers who have completed the stretching exercises at the end of each chapter are now well prepared to consider the method of time management we are about to discuss. You have established a Pro-Vision™. You have identified your Pro-Values™. You have set long-term goals in each of the major playing fields of your life. Now, it's time to begin achieving those goals, and that is accomplished day by day, hour by hour, minute by minute. Your plan must be mapped out, and kept constantly in front of you, or the goal will get lost in the demands of the urgent-but-not-always-vital.

Mine is a two-part method. Step one involves the preparation of a single index card.

	Daily	1 year	5 years	10 years
Soul				
Body				
Mind				
Love				
Peer				
Work				

Player's Box

Now it's time to fill in the blanks.

	Daily	1 year	5 years	10 years
Soul	Bible - 30 min.	5 people	10 people	50 people
Body	6 x a week	15% body fat	maintain level	continue to lift
Mind	reduce tv, read	write book	produce bk tape	international bk
Love	family time	"date" each one	trip to Prague	trip to Australia
Peer	smile first	new friend	deepen	5 new friends
Work	learn new	share it - locally	share it - world	be a mentor

Notice that I've used abbreviations for my goals: just something to remind me of what they are. Looking at the long-term goals helps me decide what I need to do daily to accomplish them. I fill in the daily column last.

These, for example, are the goals I want to pursue in the Soul column: reading my Bible at least 30 minutes a day, sharing what I know about Christ with at least five people this year, at least 10 people annually within five years, and at least 50 people annually within 10 years.

In the Body column, I'm reminding myself to exercise at least six times a week, maintain 15% body fat for the next five years, and continue to lift weights even when I'm 60! The other columns follow the same pattern.

Part two of my method involves a daily planner. I've been accused of being fanatical about the use of these, but I have never known a more useful tool. Years ago, I purchased a leather bound pocket-sized Day-Timer that I've turned into my

Player's Box

wallet. My driver's license, important papers and money are always with me. The monthly calendar lets me know exactly where I plan to be over the next several months.

But the daily planning pages are the real workhorses of my system. I use a single-page-per-day planner. Each page is broken down into hourly segments. I split the page in half. The left half is where I record appointments (using a pencil, not a pen, in case I need to make changes) and the right half is a list of things to be done that day.

The concept for how I use my Day-Timer dates to before the turn of the century when, the story goes, a management consultant named Ivey Lee was hired by steel tycoon Charles Schwab (great grandfather of today's stockbroker-entrepreneur of the same name.) Schwab asked Lee to give him a technique for using his time better. Lee asked Schwab to write down everything he had to do the next day. Next, Schwab was to look at the list in its entirety and write a number one beside the most critical task to be done the next day. All others were to be ranked numerically by importance, as well. Lee then instructed Schwab to work on the number one task until he had done as much as he could to complete it before moving to the next task. When Schwab asked how much he owed Lee for the concept, Lee replied to the effect of, "Try the method for a month and then send me what you think it's worth." At the end of the month, Lee received a check for $25,000 — and this was in the

Player's Box

days before income tax!

I use a slightly more complex system. Either the previous night or early each morning, I assign the capital letters A or B to each item on my to-do list. An A means the action absolutely has to be done that day. B items are those that would be nice to do, but are not critical on that particular day. B items can be carried over or dropped, but not an A.

I then rank the items on my A list, using Mr. Lee's method. That tells me the order in which I'll begin work each day. As a shorthand method, I also use a lower-case notation system at the end of each entry on my to-do list. These include

c = call
d = do a task; get something, such as "get book today"
p = pray
w = write
bc = mail birthday card
ac = mail anniversary card

My routine starts every morning at 5:30 with a brisk three-mile walk, when I also pray. I have breakfast, do my Bible study, and if I have time, read the paper quickly. My Day-Timer catches up with me at 7:00. Here's a sample day:

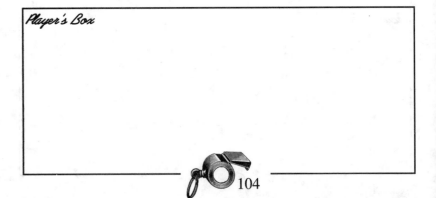

Player's Box

7 Weight lifting	B3 c - Billy
8 Shower	A4 w - Steve on contract
9 Margaret - there	A2 w - Final report
10	B2 c - Margaret
11 Brett - there	A3 bc - John Singleman
12 Steve and Cindy - Cafe	
1	A1 p - Connie's operation
2 IBM - Cindy - there	
3	
4 Phone time	
5:30 Kelly - baseball	
6 Dinner	
7 Zoe	
8 Zach's homework	
9 Read	
10 Bed	

Psalm 90:17 May the favor of the Lord our God rest upon us; establish the work of our hands for us - yes, establish the work of our hands.

Remember that the left hand side of the page is for appointments, either with others or with myself. The right-hand side is a reminder list. For example, on this particular day, when a friend is having surgery, I consider it a top priority to pray for

Player's Box

her, so I've labeled that "p" item number 1. The item I've ranked as A2 is marked with a "w" to remind me that, after praying for Connie, I should get started writing the final report from a project with an upcoming deadline.

If you're not careful, your daily pages will reflect a life that's out of balance. You may notice that the vast majority of your appointments fall into one or two categories, rather than being spread among all six categories of the Life Pre-Server™.

For that reason, I intentionally block out at least one segment of time per day for each segment of my Life Pre-Server™.

Because every other segment radiates from the "Soul Hole," I start with that. My daily soul goal is to spend at least 30 minutes systematically reading through the Bible. If I don't schedule it as an appointment, that time will most certainly get swallowed up by other things. The same concept applies to physical exercise. Sometimes people ask me to meet them for a meal and ask me if I'm busy at a particular time. I tell them I already have a pre-scheduled appointment at that time. I don't necessarily have to explain that my appointment is to work out. I've found that if I don't schedule that time, someone inevitably takes it from me, or I give it away. Then, I'm mad with myself because I didn't work out that day.

I block in time to spend with my wife and my children, by name, making it a point to set a special "date" with each of my

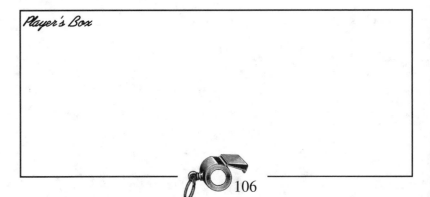

Player's Box

106

four children at least once a month. Based on the Lord's promptings during my prayer time, I'm likely to write, call or schedule lunch with a friend. I tend to read at least four library books at a time, and if I haven't had any reading time during the day, I substitute reading for television in the evenings.

At the bottom of my daily planner page, I have room to write a Scripture verse from my daily Bible reading. The verse I select is one that seems to speak directly to me or to the circumstances I may find myself in that day. I refer back to it during the day, and I'm often struck by how applicable and timely the verse is for the circumstances that have cropped up since that early morning devotional time.

Another use for my daily planner is to record those matters people ask me to pray for. One of the gifts I think the Lord has given me is to be sensitive to the needs of others. I often ask people how I can pray for them. Some people are stunned; they really don't know what to say. Other people recognize that I'm sincere, and will truly tell me something on their heart that I can pray about. I record it in my Day-Timer in the right hand column under things to do. That evening I transfer the request to a larger prayer sheet that I keep in my Bible. That way, I know I will pray for that person once a week for at least a year. The prayer sheet is also a great way of keeping a journal of how the Lord is working in my life.

Player's Box

STUDYING THE CLIPS:

Michael Wasson was a fine high school football player. He played on the 11 and 0 conference team I coached in 1980, in which we set team goals for each quarter of every game, as well as personal goals for each player. We even had a Pro-Vision™ back then for the team. It came from Mark Rockefeller, an all-star end. Whenever Mark ran wind sprints at the end of practice he ran faster and faster with each sprint. I asked him how he did it and he quoted Philippians 4:13. "I can do all things through Christ." That was our Pro-Vision™ for the season! After Michael's graduation we lost contact with each other. Then I received an invitation to his graduation from dental school! He and his wife set up practice in Asheville, NC. Having introduced him to using a daily planner back in high school, I was pleased to see he's still using it today. He says it helps him stay focused both in his practice and his personal life with Etta Marie and their two boys, Rees and Benjamin. What a joy to see how the Lord has worked in his life and in the lives of his family!

Player's Box

STRETCHING EXERCISE:

If you're using a month-at-a-glance calendar that gives you a one-inch square to write down your day's plans, face the fact that you can't plan a day in an inch. Office supply stores are full of daily planners. Your stretching exercise is to buy one that you'll now be experimenting with. It can be a paper version like mine, or a high-tech computerized notebook, but it needs to be something you can carry with you everywhere you go. Remember it takes at least 21 days to make a habit change, so you may need to stick with your planner at least three weeks before you start appreciating all it can do for you.

TEAM STRETCHING EXERCISE:

Compare the types of daily planners you're using. Discuss why it is it so hard to get people to budget their time wisely.

FOCAL POINT:

"There is a time for everything, and a season for every activity under the heaven." Ecclesiastes 3:1

Player's Box

Chapter 14
Counterclockwise or Clockwise?

THE CHALK TALK:

In most of the world's racing events, are the participants running in a clockwise or counterclockwise direction? It's an interesting question, and one you may not have considered before.

Think about it. NASCAR races, Indy races, horse and dog races, even Olympic track races are all run ... counterclockwise! The one exception I know of is the steeplechase in England — an appropriate exception we'll discuss a little later.

If we look at our Life Pre-Server™ in terms of direction and priorities, we can see how most adults run their lives in a counterclockwise manner. As soon as we get out of high school or college, most people place their primary focus on getting (1) a job. Moving counterclockwise, they connect with adult (2) peers. From that peer group usually comes an attraction to a potential mate — a marriage partner, the (3) love relationship. Since, at this point, most of us have neither distilled our direction into a Pro-Vision™, nor established our Pro-Values™, the seeds for failure and disappointment have already been sown. Because things are probably backing up at work or at home, we have little time for our (4) mind, (5) body and most critically, our (6) soul.

Player's Box

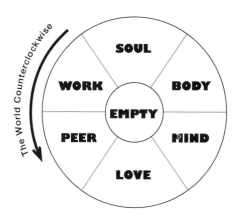

We are now running a never-ending, never rewarding race I call the "Hamster Shuffle." The faster we run, the tired-er we get. We never seem to have any time to ourselves. There just aren't enough hours in the day. And this goes on day after exhausting day, with no end in sight. Just like our family hamsters running in their wheels all night long, these people never go anywhere, and it sure is exhausting to watch them work.

Sound familiar? Now, let's look at life from a different perspective — not from a counterclockwise view, as the rest of the world does it, but from an orderly, clockwise Pro-Vision™, Pro-Values™, Life Pre-Server™ perspective.

Player's Box

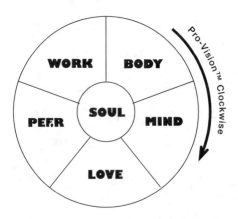

Life Pre-Server™

This perspective starts with (1) the soul. If you can truthfully say you know God, then you will be asking God to guide you, as together, you develop your personal Pro-Vision™ and Pro-Values™. You then establish some well thought-out soul-goals, and because you have started in the rightful center of your life, you will step out into the rest of life from a position of strength.

If you do not know God, seeking Him is the only soul-goal you need. Be honest as you pray. If you don't know God, tell him so. Ask Him to reveal himself. Begin reading his great play-book, the Bible. Remember, you are truly Pre-Serving your life!

Now, we move from the center of the Life Pre-Server™ to the outer ring. We commit ourselves to taking care of (2) the

Player's Box

body — the only one we have. Since the body is inextricably linked to its center, the soul, we must consider the relationship between them. The Bible calls the body "the temple of the Holy Spirit," and the temple must be cared for. Here, we should set achievable goals.

Next, we examine what we are allowing to invade our personal computer — (3) the mind. The intellect must be cultivated, or it becomes flabby, incapable of reasoning. There are achievable goals to be set here as well. Do the spiritual and the intellectual touch? Yes, the Bible says its words actually renew our minds!

The next stop on the clockwise path is the area of (4) human love. Love needs to start with you. If you don't love yourself in a realistic way, appreciating your value as a one-of-a-kind human being created especially by God, how will you know how to love someone else? How can you love your neighbor if you don't love yourself? Human love reaches its zenith when the partners are first united soul-to-soul by a common belief in Jesus Christ.

Then we move on to (5) peers. We look for peers who share our values, not peers who work to tear them down. The Bible's Book of Proverbs has much to say about the value and the pleasure of having a good friend — and the dangers of having a bad one.

And finally in this clockwise journey, we come to our (6)

Player's Box

work. It is to be enjoyed, in the same way that God took obvious pleasure in his creative work described in Genesis 1. We are emulating God when we enjoy an honorable job well done.

By moving counter to the direction the world moves, we gain what the world wants in the first place: joy, springing from the soul and moving through the body, the mind, the heart, our relationships, and the work we do!

I mentioned the steeplechase earlier. Unlike the world's other races, it moves clockwise. Its very name points us toward heaven. God's way always runs counter to the world's way, and ultimately, His is always the right way.

Run your race with purpose, never losing sight of your Pro-Vision™, Pro-Values™ or Life Pre-Server™. Let all your goals contribute to your successful arrival at that finish line. Run as though your life depends on it (it does!) Run against the world — run clockwise, not counterclockwise!

Player's Box

STRETCHING EXERCISE:

Do you want to run your life's race, clockwise or counter-clockwise? List the changes do you need to make to begin running your life in a clockwise manner.

TEAM STRETCHING EXERCISE:

Discuss your own experience in running the "Hamster Shuffle." Which sections of your life tend to get lost in the shuffle?

FOCAL POINT:

"Trust in the Lord with all your heart; lean not on your own understanding. In all your ways acknowledge Him, and He will make your paths straight." Proverbs 3: 5-6

Player's Box

Chapter 15
My Life

I was born on Valentine's Day, 1947, in Washington, D.C., on my father's twenty-eighth birthday. As a U.S. Army captain, Dad had been badly wounded in the Battle of the Bulge — shot in the stomach with a machine gun — but he packed his wounds with snow and became one of the few officers in his company to survive. My mom worked in the fingerprint division of the FBI in Washington, D.C., until the war was over.

Shortly after I was born, we began our lengthy history of traveling with the Army. By the time I was four, just before the development of the Salk vaccine, the polio epidemic was sweeping the world. Several passengers on the transport ship that took Mom and me to meet Dad in Puerto Rico contracted polio and died. A week after we docked, I contracted it, too, and spent months and months in the hospital, wearing leg braces and learning how to walk all over again. Despite the damage done to my leg muscles, I threw myself into the great love of my young life — sports. So did my three younger brothers, Jeff, Frank and Jim.

Dad came from a Catholic background, while my mother was raised a Southern Baptist. I grew up attending Army churches, and during the time that my father was an ROTC instructor at several colleges in Southern California, we at

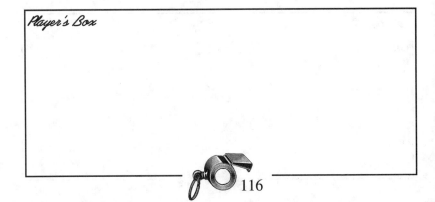

Player's Box

tended a Baptist church in the community.

There, I learned all the right things to say. I memorized Scripture. Just about everybody I knew was involved in some kind of church activity — even the Boy Scouts, who met at an Episcopal Church. But my heart was disengaged. During my teenage years, I saw people in church who, I felt, were acting hypocritically — adults telling off-color jokes during a youth retreat, for example. That distanced me even more from God.

Even in high school, I exercised certain standards of self-discipline, and one of my strongest personal values was my refusal to drink or do anything else that would adversely affect my ability to play sports. I was already handicapped by my thick glasses, my skinny frame, and the atrophied muscles in my right leg. I wasn't going to do anything else to hurt my performance on the playing field. I refused to even walk into a bar.

During my high school days, Dad was stationed at Ft. Jackson in Columbia, SC. In Columbia, I began dating Zoe Ann. The day after my graduation in 1965, my family flew to Germany, where my father was assigned as a base commander in Stuttgart. I started college in Munich, and it was there, in a culture that celebrated the making and drinking of beer, that I changed my values. Rationalizing that I needed to put on weight, I started drinking very high alcohol content German beer, and I liked it. I liked the way it made me feel. It took away a lot of my inhibitions, especially about being around

Player's Box

girls. In my partying lifestyle, I was now totally turned away from God.

In 1966, I transferred to the University of Kentucky, where in December of 1969, I graduated with a BA degree in Physical Sciences. My plan was to teach chemistry and coach football in Southern California; in fact, I had the job lined up. But about that time, my mother became very sick. Dad was in Korea at the time, and Mother had moved back to Ft. Jackson. So I cancelled my plans and stayed in Columbia, taking a job with Allied Signal Corporation as a quality control shift foreman. I also began dating Zoe Ann again. By now, she had graduated from Breneau College in Georgia, and was getting her master's degree. I proposed to her once, but broke the engagement over a disagreement with her parents. We didn't see each other for eight months. At the end of that time, I knew that Zoe Ann was really my best friend, and that I needed her in my life. I asked if she would consider eloping. I was still not going to church or living a Christian life, and I knew it would be hypocritical of me to get married in a church. Besides, I was never one for big, formal ceremonies. Zoe Ann agreed, and we were married in April 1971, to the great consternation of her parents, who forbade us to come home.

In July, Allied offered me a job in its marketing department on Times Square in New York City. While working in New York, I earned my MBA in marketing from Fordham

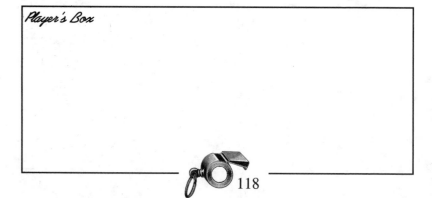

Player's Box

118

University in 1974. Life was exciting there. My two middle brothers had been accepted to West Point, only about 75 miles away, and Zoe Ann and I spent football weekends at West Point.

Zoe Ann had been raised in an Episcopal family, and she continued to go to church. I mocked her faith. At times, I would accompany her to her Bible study, bombard the rector with questions, express all my doubts about Christianity and the truth of the Bible, and generally act obnoxious. But I was faithful to Zoe Ann. I had promised her that we would move back down South, and now, learning that her mother was dying of breast cancer, I was determined to make the move.

It was the middle of the Arab oil embargo, and good jobs were hard to find, especially in the South. Allied offered me a job as a process engineer in the plant, working 12 hours a day on a rotating shift. Despite the fact that I am a non-mechanical person, I misrepresented my abilities and took the job just to come back South. I really didn't like it. Zoe Ann had become pregnant, and I — who had enjoyed my life as it was and never wanted children — was very upset. I asked her to have an abortion and she refused. She started going to another Episcopal church and was drawing real strength from that. I asked her to give me a divorce. She said no.

I was miserable. She was miserable. I would climb up on the fifth floor of the manufacturing building where I worked, make my way to the edge of the roof and consider jumping —

Player's Box

I was just so miserable with my job, my wife, and my life. I drowned it all several nights a week by going out with the guys and getting drunk, but time after time, I came back to the roof. Thank God I never had the guts to jump off, and that He kept me safe.

In May of 1975, a former boss, who knew I was struggling, asked if I would meet with a friend of his, a Presbyterian minister who was a former basketball coach. So every Wednesday afternoon for the next three months, I would go to the Presbyterian Church and meet with Bill Solomon. I poured my heart out to Bill, told him how miserable I was, told him about all the hypocrisy I had seen in the church, and how I believed you couldn't prove the Bible was true. He was gracious enough to listen and share Scripture with me, but never pushed me. He knew I wasn't open to that yet.

For three months, Bill just let me wallow in my misery, encouraging me to talk it out, being a great listener. I gave him all of my excuses why I couldn't become a Christian. It wasn't that I disagreed with the premise that I was a sinner. I was in total agreement with that. It wasn't that I didn't understand what Christ had done for me. I totally understood that He had willingly taken the punishment I deserved for my sins, allowing me to be forgiven. I understood that the only other eternal option was hell. I just wasn't willing to give in. I wanted the ultimate control of my life.

Player's Box

It's difficult for a man to give up his independence, especially when you've been raised all your life to be an independent person, when you've come to believe that you can do anything you want without God. It's especially hard to give the control of your life to someone else, especially a spiritual someone, whom you can't even see. But on August 10, 1975, I ran out of excuses, and Bill asked me what I was going to do now. I told him it looked like I was going to have to accept Christ on His terms, and not mine. That was the turning point. You've got to come to the realization that all the excuses you throw up are just that — excuses. You've got to come to Christ as a child does — with childlike faith that he can give you a whole new life.

I got down on my knees with Bill beside me. He read through a booklet put out by Campus Crusade for Christ, outlining four spiritual laws, which are just as valid as the physical laws of gravity and thermodynamics.

I agreed with each of the four laws. Bill read a prayer of faith, repentance and commitment, asked me how I felt about it, and asked if I would like to pray a similar prayer. That afternoon, I turned my life and my direction over to Christ.

I didn't share that news with Zoe Ann for several days. There were no bells and whistles going off inside me. It was a simple transfer of ownership of my life. On the fifteenth, Zoe Ann's mother died of breast cancer. Zoe Ann was devastated. I

Player's Box

got out the Bible and just started reading Scripture. Zoe Ann was shocked, and that's when I shared with her that I had become a Christian. The Lord really worked in my life from that point on — and has never stopped.

Not all of His work was accomplished immediately, nor was it always pleasant to endure. For example, I continued to hate my work, and knew that it was dishonest of me to continue to draw a paycheck when I was not performing up to the company's standards. In September of '76, I was fired from Allied, and emotionally and intellectually, I had to work through that. I had believed that if you became a Christian, only good things happened to you. (That misguided theology had not come from Bill Solomon, but my own lack of understanding. What I didn't realize was that God could use even bad or unpleasant things for good in the lives of his children.)

Neither had I stopped drinking. I rationalized that since Jesus turned water into wine at a wedding, that allowed me to continue to drink — heavily. By this time, I was coaching middle school football, and my drinking affected my credibility as a Christian with the players and their parents. In April 1977, Bill Solomon was preaching on I Corinthians 10:31: "Whatsoever you eat or drink, or whatever you do, do it all to the glory of God." It seemed phenomenal to me that he could devote an entire sermon to that one verse, but by the end of it, I felt as if

Player's Box

all the breath had been knocked out of me. I knew God had spoken to me through that verse and that sermon, and I knew I had to give up drinking. That's when I spent an entire Sunday afternoon pouring bottles and cases of alcohol down the drain. This verse became my Pro-Vision™.

I worked with Nautilus Fitness Centers in exercise training, marketing, and management for four years, with a two-year break in the middle to become coach at Thornwell Children's Home. In 1983, the Lord gave me the opportunity to combine two passions: teaching and coaching. I became a marketing professor at Coastal Carolina University in Conway, SC, while also working in the athletic department as its strength coach. In 1987, I also resumed work on my Ph.D. in higher education administration, with a major in marketing. I received my degree from the University of South Carolina in 1991. The administration at Coastal decided to pursue accreditation from the American Association of Collegiate Schools of Business and told me my degree would not qualify. In May of 1995, I was notified that I would have six more months at Coastal. Here was another example of an apparent catastrophe working out for good in the hands of God.

The Lord opened up the opportunity for me to form a company called The Coach's Corner. The Coach's Corner allows me to combine my coaching background, my business background, and my academic background into one role. We

Player's Box

123

do corporate educational programs for private companies and government agencies, covering the same areas described in this book. The business really belongs to the Lord. He brings me all my clients! I thank Him every day for the opportunity to see the miracles He provides in our lives.

Zoe Ann and I have been married 26 years. We have four children. We are members of a great church — Myrtle Beach Community Church. The pastor there, Ronny Byrd, reminds me a lot of Bill Solomon.

Our oldest daughter, Carrie, is 22. She just graduated from Coastal with a degree in English and is working in the marketing field in Myrtle Beach. Jenny is 20, a rising senior and history major at Coastal. She wants to teach on the college level.

Kelly is 12, a very bright student and a great softball player. She has such a gift of taking care of people. I wouldn't be surprised if she became a doctor or a nurse. And 10-year-old Zach — we've gone through a lot with him, almost losing him to meningitis at six months old. Defying the doctors' predictions that, if he lived, he would be brain damaged and crippled, Zach is our "miracle child" — a very good student and a truly gifted athlete.

I really enjoy coaching Kelly and Zach in their various sports. Spending time with the family is probably the greatest joy in my life. I also tremendously enjoy the opportunities I

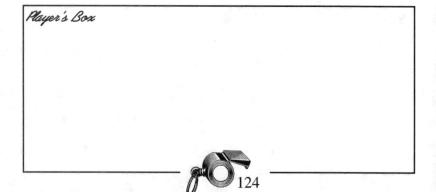

Player's Box

124

have to tell others about Christ. As a family we continue to be active in the Fellowship of Christian Athletes.

Prayer is the glue that keeps me focused. It's nice to be in a special quiet place to pray, but you can pray anywhere — standing up with your eyes open. I would encourage anyone who is taking this journey to make prayer a constant part of your life. It is so freeing to take any worry or concern you have about anything to the Lord in prayer. Then you need to learn to leave the prayer request with Him. Don't take it back just to have something to worry about. That's one of Satan's great temptations. He wants you to take your prayer requests back and worry about them. How sad! Leave them with the One you have placed your trust in - not yourself. He is powerful - the most powerful force in the universe. Just do it - just believe in Him.

Now, the Lord has brought Bill Solomon full circle in my life. Margaret and I prayed about finding an editor who was a Christian and athletically minded to review our work. Bill graciously agreed and in his wisdom, suggested we add the Team Stretching Exercises to each chapter, in order to be useful to groups.

Our prayer is that our readers will find these *notes from the Coach* a playbook that points them consistently to our great head coach and his eternal playbook, the Bible.

Player's Box

FOCAL POINT:

" Where there are no oxen, the manger is empty, but from the strength of an ox comes an abundant harvest."
Proverbs 14:4

Player's Box

For further information on speaking
engagements or additional books

Contact:
Dr. Ed Cerny
148 Citadel Dr.
Conway, SC 29526
1-800-681-4231
e-mail winners@ns1.sccoast.net

Player's Box

Player's Box

128